Building the Kingdom
Through the Local Church

David Webb

Cover designed by EKI Publishing

Printed in the United States of America

First Printing: July 2025

Eternal Kingdom International Publishing, LLC

LIBRARY OF CONGRESS

Library of Congress Control Number: 2025948331

ISBN- 978-1-968815-06-6 - Paperback

ISBN- 978-1-968815-07-3 - Hardback

ISBN- 978-1-968815-08-0 - eBook

Other Works by David Webb:

- *Escape The Shame of Babylon* EKI Publishing 2025

- *The Unique Factor* EKI Publishing 2025

The prophet that hath a dream, let him tell a dream; and he that hath my word, let him speak my word faithfully. What *is* the chaff to the wheat? saith the LORD. *Is* not my word like as a fire? saith the LORD; and like a hammer *that* breaketh the rock in pieces?

- Jeremiah 23: 28-29 (KJV)

Dedication:

I dedicate this book to the faithful voices - my friends and mentors - who urged me to write, who believed there was a message worth preserving in ink. I dedicate it also to my children and grandchildren, that they may one day read and walk in the inheritance of these words.

I dedicate it to my Pastor, whose request stirred me to begin. For though this book now stands complete, other manuscripts have been assembled quietly in the background over the years, waiting for their appointed time, fulfilling the charge laid upon me.

.

David Webb

Introduction

The Call That Still Builds

Before there was a pulpit, there was an altar. Before there was a crowd, there was a covenant. And before there was a church, there was a cry in the heart of God - *"Let us make man in Our image."* (Genesis 1:26) That cry was not the sound of religion; it was the sound of relationship. It was heaven's decree that the earth would host a dwelling for God - a people, not a program; a body, not a brand; a living temple where glory would not visit but abide.

From Eden to the wilderness, from the tent of meeting to the temple of Solomon, God's desire has been consistent: to dwell among His people. But the story does not end with a temple of stone - it ends with a city of light. John saw it and wrote, *"And I saw a new heaven and a new earth… and I heard a great voice out of heaven saying, Behold, the tabernacle of God is with men, and He will dwell with them, and they shall be His people, and God Himself shall be with them, and be their God."* (Revelation 21:1–3)

This is the final vision of all creation - the union of heaven and earth, the divine dream fulfilled. Jesus declared, *"Heaven and earth shall pass away, but My words shall not pass away."* (Matthew 24:35) Everything temporary will give way to the eternal Word. And when the old order dissolves, what remains will be what the Word has built - His Church, His Bride, His dwelling among men.

The prophets foresaw it long before John beheld it: *"For, behold, I create new heavens and a new earth: and the former shall not be remembered."* (Isaiah 65:17) *"Nevertheless we, according to His promise, look for new heavens and a new earth, wherein dwelleth righteousness."* (2 Peter 3:13)

The local church, therefore, is not a man-made institution - it is the earthly rehearsal of the eternal reality. It is the preview of the world to come, where God's sons and daughters rule and reign with Him - not in mansions in heaven, but on the redeemed earth, where the glory of God fills every nation and light has no end. The building we raise today foreshadows the Kingdom we will inhabit forever.

A Kingdom Blueprint

The local church is heaven's construction site. It is the proving ground where believers are not just inspired but transformed, not entertained but equipped. Here, spectators become soldiers, and the milk of convenience gives way to the meat of conviction. Here, sons and daughters are trained for battle, not to wave banners of culture but to carry the standard of the King.

We have built enough stages; it is time to build altars. We have measured success by attendance, while heaven measures by obedience.

The Spirit of God is shaking the foundations of every shallow model that substituted applause for authority. God is tearing down audience-driven religion and raising up Kingdom-centered families. For the Kingdom is not in word only - but in power (1 Corinthians 4:20).

This is not a book for the passive believer. It is for those who feel the rumble of divine dissatisfaction in their bones - those who know there must be more than polished sermons and empty hands. It is for builders, not watchers; for fathers and mothers, not mere instructors; for those who carry a burden for the house of God as Nehemiah did when he said, *"Let us rise up and build."* (Nehemiah 2:18)

A Family That Becomes an Army

Every revival that shaped history was birthed not by crowds but by covenant. Abram's house began as a family - but when Lot was captured, that family became an army. *"And when Abram heard that his brother [relative, nephew (Lot)]was taken captive, he armed his trained servants, born in his own house, three hundred and eighteen, and pursued them."* (Genesis 14:14)

That is the picture of the Church God is restoring - an apostolic family, trained, disciplined, and spiritually armed to rescue the captive, confront darkness, and reclaim territory for the King. And that same army, perfected through obedience and endurance, will one day stand as the radiant Bride in the New Jerusalem, a family fully revealed upon the new earth where the

Father Himself dwells among His children. *"For the earnest expectation of the creature waiteth for the manifestation of the sons of God."* (Romans 8:19)

Creation groans, not for escape, but for revelation - the unveiling of mature sons and daughters who will reign with Christ in a restored creation.

The enemy fears one thing above all: a united church filled with the Holy Ghost. He doesn't tremble at our programs, our conferences, or our logos - he trembles when believers discover who they are. When the Church moves in its divine identity as God's habitation, hell loses jurisdiction. When pastors lead as fathers, elders nurture as mothers, and believers function as sons and soldiers, the Kingdom advances with unstoppable force.

The Builders' Mandate

This book is a trumpet call to those who refuse to play church. It is a summons to builders - apostles, prophets, teachers, pastors, deacons, intercessors, and saints - who sense the Spirit of the Lord whispering, "Build again." For too long we have confused motion with momentum, growth with greatness, and comfort with calling. But the Lord of the Harvest is searching for wise master builders who will lay again the foundation of Christ, who will restore apostolic order, prophetic fire, and shepherding love.

Paul said, *"According to the grace given unto me, as a wise master builder, I have laid the foundation…"* (1 Corinthians 3:10). Grace is not a feeling - it is divine architecture. And every local church that survives the shaking to come must be built on that blueprint: Christ the cornerstone, apostolic foundation, prophetic alignment, and the training of saints for Kingdom purpose.

To build this way is to participate in the new creation already unfolding. Each obedient act, each disciple raised, each family restored, is a prophetic rehearsal of Revelation 21. The Church on earth is building toward the City of God - *"prepared as a bride adorned for her husband."*

The Coming Reformation

The days ahead will separate the churches that can host glory from those that can only host gatherings. The next revival will not be televised; it will be localized. It will not come through celebrities but through communities - ordinary believers ignited by extraordinary vision. It will flow through local churches that become embassies of heaven in every city, every nation, every generation.

For the Lord is not building cathedrals of comfort; He is building command centers of conquest. He is transforming families into armies, audiences into disciples, and gatherings into government. The Spirit is whispering again, "The time to build has come."

And when the last stone is set and the Bride is complete, the voice John heard will sound again: *"Behold, the tabernacle of God is with men."*

No longer will the presence of God be confined to temples or revivals, for the dwelling of God will fill the redeemed earth. Here, the sons and daughters will walk in unveiled glory. Here, the family of God will reign under the eternal Word whose throne endures when heaven and earth have passed away. For what we build now in obedience becomes the framework of eternity.

So, lift your eyes, builder of the Kingdom. The blueprints of heaven are being released again. Your hammer is your obedience. Your nails are your prayers. And your materials are the living stones sitting beside you. The foundation has been laid. The call has gone forth. Now heaven waits for your answer.

Will you rise and build?

Contents

Prelude

The King's Blueprint

Before there was a sermon, there was a sound. Before there was a congregation, there was a covenant. Before there was a church, there was a Kingdom.

In the beginning, God did not design a religion - He released a realm. The Kingdom of Heaven was the original order, a living government flowing from His throne, like *"a pure river of water of life, clear as crystal, proceeding out of the throne of God and of the Lamb"* (Revelation 22:1). It was a realm where life itself streamed from the very seat of divine authority, ruled by His Word and carried by His image-bearers. Every act of creation was an architectural decree. The heavens declared His glory; the earth displayed His design. Man was not created to attend a service, but to host His presence - to be the living sanctuary of the Almighty in the midst of creation.

When man fell, heaven did not abandon earth - it began to build again. From the ruins of rebellion, the Father drafted a new blueprint of redemption. Every covenant was a construction phase, every prophet a builder, every apostle a foreman of destiny. The altar of Abraham, the tabernacle of Moses, the temple of

Solomon - all were foundations pointing to something greater. Then came the Master Builder Himself - Christ, the Son of the Living God - declaring, *"Upon this rock I will build My Church, and the gates of hell shall not prevail against it."* (Matthew 16:18)

The local church, therefore, is not an invention of man; it is the continuation of that divine construction. It is the visible blueprint of the invisible Kingdom. It is the training ground where sons and daughters are forged into builders, where family becomes army, and where obedience becomes architecture. Every sermon is a stone. Every act of discipleship, a beam. Every transformed life, a wall rising toward heaven's vision.

The Pattern of the Builder

Every generation is tested by whether it will preserve the pattern. Heaven's designs are never suggestions; they are sacred trust. Moses was warned, *"See that thou make all things according to the pattern shewed to thee in the mount."* (Hebrews 8:5) Paul echoed that same call: *"As a wise master builder, I have laid the foundation."* (1 Corinthians 3:10)

The pattern has not changed. Apostles and prophets lay the foundation. Evangelists, pastors, and teachers build upon it. Each member of the body fits together as living stones, chosen and shaped by the hand of the Builder Himself. When the pattern is followed, the glory fills the house. When it is ignored, Ichabod is written over the door.

This is why the enemy wages his fiercest war against the local church. He fears not our gatherings, but our unity. He trembles when the people of God build in order, aligned with apostolic blueprints and prophetic fire. Babylon builds towers to make names for men; Zion builds temples to reveal the name of the King. One is confusion; the other is glory. One ends in scattering; the other ends in habitation.

The true church is not a monument to human achievement but a movement of divine government. Its leaders are not executives but fathers and mothers. Its members are not customers but soldiers of covenant. The church exists not to host performances but to host Presence - because when God dwells among His people, every power of darkness begins to crumble.

The Mandate to Build

The Spirit of the Lord is issuing the same command that stirred Nehemiah's heart in ancient ruins: *"Let us rise up and build."* (Nehemiah 2:18)

This is not a suggestion for the talented - it is a mandate for the obedient. Heaven is not impressed by motion but by momentum, not by numbers but by transformation. We have built enough stages; it is time to build altars. We have measured success by attendance; heaven measures by obedience. We have polished our performances; it is time to forge disciples.

The Church is not the waiting room for heaven; it is the workshop of the Kingdom. Every act of faithfulness lays another stone. Every disciple raised strengthens another wall. Every family healed **manifests the reach of heaven's reign** on earth. The Church does not enlarge heaven; it reveals heaven's government already at work through obedient lives. When believers take their place as builders, the earth begins to mirror the government of heaven.

The blueprint is not hidden - it is written in the Word. The Cornerstone is not uncertain - it is Christ alone. The call is not for a few - it is for all who bear His name. The Kingdom will not be built by entertainment but by endurance, not by charisma but by covenant, not by applause but by alignment with heaven's pattern.

From Foundation to Fulfillment

The day is coming when the final stone will be set and the heavenly voice will thunder again: *"Behold, the tabernacle of God is with men."* (Revelation 21:3)

In that moment, every local church built in obedience will echo in eternity. Every hidden labor, every unseen prayer, every act of sacrifice will become part of the eternal architecture of the New Jerusalem. The Bride will stand complete - glorious, united, and radiant with the light of the Lamb. The King's blueprint will be finished.

So lift your eyes, builder of the Kingdom. Your hammer is your obedience. Your nails are your prayers. Your material is the living stones sitting beside you. The foundation has been laid, and the Cornerstone holds firm.

The voice of the Builder still calls through time: *"Rise up and build."* For what you build now will stand when heaven and earth have passed away. The kingdoms of men will crumble, but the Kingdom built through the local church will endure forever.

Chapter One

The Call to Build – Why the Local Church is Central to the Kingdom

Introduction

From the beginning, God has always had a dwelling place among His people. In the beginning, it was a garden. In the wilderness, it was the tabernacle. In Jerusalem, it was the temple. But in this age, His habitation is the ekklesia - the Church - built upon the foundation of apostles and prophets, with Jesus Christ Himself as the chief cornerstone (Ephesians 2:20). The local church is not an afterthought, not a side project, and not merely a place for religious services. It is the central hub of Kingdom expansion in the earth. It is through the local church that God gathers, equips, trains, and releases His people as a family that becomes an army.

The call to build is not the call to entertain. We are not summoned to gather crowds for religious performances. We are called to build communities where transformation takes root and disciples are forged in fire. The Kingdom of God is not an audience; it is an advancing force that breaks through the gates of hell. Jesus declared: "Upon this rock I will build my church, and the gates of hell shall not prevail against it" (Matthew 16:18).

Every generation faces the temptation to drift into shallow models of growth - programs that measure success by numbers rather than by transformation. But the Spirit of God is declaring again: "Milk makes an audience; meat makes an army." The Kingdom does not call us to build stages for spectators; it summons us to raise soldiers for battle.

God's Design: The Church as His Dwelling Place

Paul describes the church as a holy temple in the Lord, a dwelling place of God through the Spirit (Ephesians 2:21–22). This means the church is not just a meeting but a habitation. It is a structure where living stones are fitly framed together, each believer carrying divine purpose and assignment.

Genesis 14 reveals Abram raising up a household of trained servants, a prophetic picture of God's vision for His people. Abram's family was not a passive audience but an equipped force: *"And when Abram heard that his brother [relative, nephew (Lot)]was taken captive, he armed his trained servants, born in his own house, three hundred and eighteen, and pursued them"* (Genesis 14:14). The local church is meant to function in the same way - a family first, but then a family trained and armed for battle.

This is why the prophetic declaration rings true: A family that becomes an army. The end goal is never an audience. Babies cannot live on their own, and spiritual infants must be raised into maturity. Every believer enters as a newborn, but God's desire is that they grow to full stature in Christ.

When the church neglects this process, it produces weak followers tethered to someone else's faith. But when the church trains its people, it releases disciples who are ready to confront darkness. Training is what transforms a congregation from an audience of dependents into an army of overcomers.

Audience-Driven or Kingdom-Focused

Modern church culture often measures success by the size of its gatherings rather than the maturity of its saints. Crowds are drawn by performance, style, and marketing, but God is not impressed with numbers. He looks for transformation.

Here the prophetic warning cuts deep: These models are more into advertising than anointing. They will tell you that if you want to grow the church, get into advertising. You may catch them, but you won't keep them - because they are coming to be transformed.

Audience-driven churches prize attendance; Kingdom-focused churches prize discipleship. Audiences applaud; armies advance. Audiences come to be entertained; armies come to be trained. The church that bows to the idol of audience will produce shallow believers, but the church that bows to the King will produce soldiers who can stand in the evil day.

Paul rebuked the Corinthians for remaining on milk when they should have been eating meat: *"I have fed you with milk, and not with meat: for hitherto ye were not able to bear it"* (1 Corinthians 3:2). Milk is borrowed strength, dependent on someone else's walk. Meat is revelation chewed and digested until it becomes spiritual strength within.

The Kingdom vision is not to fill pews but to raise sons and daughters who know how to fight. It is a call to maturity. It is a call to training. It is a call to advance.

Teaching vs. Training: From Knowledge to Activation

One of the greatest dangers in the modern church is confusing teaching with training. Teaching transfers information; training produces transformation. Teaching can fill notebooks, but training fills lives with obedience, power, and purpose.

Jesus did not gather His disciples to sit in a classroom. He apprenticed them in the Kingdom. He sent them out two by two, gave them authority over unclean spirits, and required them to heal the sick, cast out demons, and proclaim the Kingdom (Mark 6:7–13). They learned by doing, not just by listening.

This is why prophetic truth declares: Teaching alone creates an audience. Training creates an army. Teaching without training produces spectators who can recite Scripture but cannot wield it. Training takes knowledge and forges it into skill.

Paul echoed this when he wrote to Timothy: *"The things that thou hast heard of me among many witnesses, the same commit thou to faithful men, who shall be able to teach others also"* (2 Timothy 2:2). Notice the multiplication: Paul taught Timothy, who trained others, who were expected to train others still. The goal was never accumulation of information but reproduction of function.

Without training, churches produce mules - strong but sterile, busy but fruitless. With training, churches reproduce leaders who can disciple nations. Without training, churches entertain. With training, churches equip. Without training, churches drift. With training, churches advance.

Foundations That Cannot Be Shaken

The local church is built upon the foundations of apostles and prophets, with Christ Jesus as the chief cornerstone (Ephesians 2:20). Apostolic and prophetic foundations establish clarity, direction, and divine order. Teachers, pastors, and evangelists then build upon what apostles and prophets lay.

Teachers, preachers, and evangelists build on top of the foundations the apostles and prophets lay. It's not the other way around. When this order is reversed, chaos erupts. But when the foundation is rightly set, the house of God becomes unshakable.

Storms will come. Cultures will rage. Nations will plot against the Lord and His anointed. Yet the church built on Christ will endure: *"Nevertheless the foundation of God standeth sure, having this seal, The Lord knoweth them that are his"* (2 Timothy 2:19). This endurance is not earned by flawless performance but secured by covenant sonship. The obedience that follows simply keeps the gates open for His power to flow.

This is why training is essential. Without apostles and prophets establishing foundation, churches drift into man-made systems that may gather people but cannot raise disciples. They may have the look of success, but their fruit will not remain. But the church anchored in Christ and aligned with apostolic and prophetic order cannot be shaken.

The Call to Rise as Builders

The call to build is not reserved for a few leaders. Every believer is summoned to take their place in God's house. Nehemiah's cry still echoes: *"Let us rise up and build. So they strengthened their hands for this good work"* (Nehemiah 2:18).

To build is to labor with vision and sacrifice. Builders do not live for applause; they live for obedience. Jesus compared them to wise men who built on rock: *"Whosoever heareth these sayings of mine, and doeth them, I will liken him unto a wise man, which built his house upon a rock"* (Matthew 7:24).

But here lies the prophetic edge: If you can't give your transparent testimony, you are fired. Leaders are not called to hide behind titles but to feed others with the testimony of their own walk. Testimony is not optional - it is food. Revelation says: *"And they overcame him by the blood of the Lamb, and by the word of their testimony"* (Revelation 12:11).

The Kingdom recognizes function, not empty titles. The work defines the man. Elder is the nature; bishop is the function. This means builders are not spectators; they are doers. They do not entertain; they train. They do not gather audiences; they raise armies.

This generation needs Nehemiahs - men and women who will rise, restore, and rebuild until the house of God stands as an unshakable fortress.

Conclusion: From Foundation to Reproduction

The call to build is the mandate of heaven for every believer. The local church is not peripheral to the Kingdom - it is central. It is here that sons and daughters are raised, trained, and sent. It is here that testimonies are birthed, gifts are sharpened, and armies are deployed.

We must reject the shallow call to gather audiences and embrace the eternal call to build God's house. For Christ is not returning for spectators but for a radiant bride, a united family, and a victorious army.

And here is a prophetic warning: strength without reproduction is failure. The mule is strong, but sterile. It can labor, but it cannot multiply. Many ministries have labored hard yet failed to reproduce. They became mules - impressive in effort, but barren in fruit. The Kingdom is not impressed with strength alone; it demands reproduction. Paul charged Timothy to entrust truth to faithful men who would entrust it to others (2 Timothy 2:2). The measure of a church is not how many it gathers but how many it sends.

"In whom all the building fitly framed together groweth unto an holy temple in the Lord: In whom ye also are builded together for an habitation of God through the Spirit" (Ephesians 2:21–22).

The call has gone out. The question remains: will you rise and build?

Scripture Index

- Ephesians 2:20–22
- Matthew 16:18 .
- Genesis 14:14
- Hebrews 5:12
- 1 Corinthians 3:2
- 2 Timothy 2:19
- Nehemiah 2:18
- Matthew 7:24
- Revelation 12:11
- Matthew 28:19
- 2 Timothy 2:2
- Mark 6:7–13

Chapter Two

A Family That Becomes an Army – From Milk Christians to Meat Christians

Introduction

The Kingdom of God is not built on spectators. It is not advanced by audiences who clap but never move. The Kingdom is carried forward by families who have been forged into armies. From the very beginning, God revealed His plan through households. Abram was not chosen because he had influence in cities or numbers in crowds; he was chosen because he would command his household after him to keep the way of the Lord (Genesis 18:19).

Every local church is meant to be more than a gathering - it is the household of faith (Galatians 6:10). Yet that household is not meant to remain in immaturity. Just as natural children grow, so must spiritual children mature. A baby cannot survive without family, and neither can a new believer survive without the church. But God's intention is not that His people remain infants, endlessly dependent on others. He intends to raise sons and daughters who will become soldiers in His Kingdom.

This is why the Spirit thunders again: A family must become an army. God is not raising audiences; He is raising warriors. He is not gathering consumers; He is forming conquerors. The destiny of the church is not to watch history unfold but to shape it through obedience and authority.

From Milk to Meat

The writer of Hebrews spoke with urgency: *"For when for the time ye ought to be teachers, ye have need that one teach you again… and are become such as have need of milk, and not of strong meat"* (Hebrews 5:12). Paul lamented to the Corinthians: *"I have fed you with milk, and not with meat: for hitherto ye were not able to bear it"* (1 Corinthians 3:2). Milk is vital for the newborn, but it is not sufficient for the mature.

There is a line that cuts to the heart of this truth: Milk makes an audience; meat makes an army. Milk keeps people dependent, endlessly entertained, and satisfied with surface understanding. Meat demands maturity. Meat requires chewing, digestion, and strength. Meat transforms children into soldiers.

No one scolds an infant for drinking milk, but if a grown man refuses to eat meat, something is tragically wrong. In the same way, the church cannot allow believers to remain in perpetual infancy. What baby can live on its own? None. So why would we expect newborn believers to survive without a family? The family of God must nurture infants, yes, but then it must also press them toward maturity until they are armed, trained, and ready for battle.

This is why discipleship cannot be confined to sermons. You can't disciple from a stage; only from a table. Teaching alone fills notebooks; discipleship fills hearts. An audience can sit quietly and applaud a message, but an army must be trained, corrected, tested, and forged.

Abram's 318: A Pattern for the Church

Genesis tells the story: *"And when Abram heard that his brother [relative, nephew (Lot)]was taken captive, he armed his trained servants, born in his own house, three hundred and eighteen, and pursued them"* (Genesis 14:14). Abram did not go to foreign nations to hire mercenaries. He turned to his household. The victory was not won by outsiders but by sons of the covenant, born in his house and trained under his authority.

This is God's pattern. Outsiders can cheer, but they cannot carry the weight of covenant. The victories of the Kingdom are entrusted to sons and daughters raised in the house, not to passing audiences. Abram's 318 were not impressive by number compared to kings and armies, but they were united, trained, and loyal. Their strength was not in size but in preparation and obedience.

So it is with the church. The measure of a church's strength is not in its seating capacity but in its sending capacity. The true power of a congregation is not in how many gather on Sunday but in how many are ready to be sent into battle for souls, justice, and truth.

Family First, Army Next

God's design has always been family first, then army. A baby cannot live on its own, and neither can a new believer. That is why the local church must begin as a family - nurturing, protecting, and feeding those who are new. But the family must not stop at the nursery. It must grow into a barracks, a place where soldiers are equipped.

An audience consumes, but an army obeys. An audience applauds, but an army advances. An audience will come and go depending on the show, but an army will stay and fight for the cause. This is why churches that are content with audiences remain shallow, while churches that raise armies shake nations.

The household of faith is not sentimental - it is strategic. Belonging gives identity, but training gives mission. God did not design the church to be a holding pen for spiritual infants. He designed it to be the factory of warriors, the family that matures into an army.

Training for Battle

Paul told Timothy, *"Thou therefore endure hardness, as a good soldier of Jesus Christ"* (2 Timothy 2:3). He did not describe Christianity as an easy stroll but as enlistment in warfare. Soldiers are not born; they are made. They are trained, disciplined, corrected, and forged.

Victory does not belong to the talented but to the trained. Victory comes not from natural strength, but from unity and obedience. One man's skill may dazzle, but it is the army's unity that wins the war. This is why local churches must train their people not just in knowledge but in discipline, prayer, and obedience to the Spirit.

Training is costly. It requires repetition, correction, and resilience. It demands that people lay aside convenience for covenant. But without training, believers are left defenseless. A church that refuses to train its people has already surrendered to the enemy.

The army of God must be skilled in intercession, sharp in discernment, grounded in the Word, and fearless in witness. We are not training performers; we are training soldiers. The battle is real, and the local church is the training ground.

From Table to Battlefield

The process begins at the table. Families gather to eat, to share, to grow. Around the table, infants are fed, children are instructed, sons are corrected, and daughters are affirmed. The table is where identity is formed. But the table is not the end. The battlefield awaits.

You can't disciple from a stage; only from a table. Stages impress, but tables transform. Stages entertain, but tables impart.

At the stage, you can create an audience. At the table, you raise an army.

The moment of testing always comes. Just as Abram's 318 were suddenly called to rescue Lot, so too the church will always face moments when it must rise. In those moments, programs will fail, advertising will not hold, and shallow religion will collapse. Only those trained at the table - those who have been corrected, equipped, and empowered - will be ready to march into the fight.

Belonging and Mission

The church must hold these two realities in tension: belonging and mission. Belonging without mission breeds complacency. Mission without belonging produces burnout. But together they form the furnace of transformation.

Belonging says, "You are family. You are loved. You are covered." Mission says, "Now rise. Now fight. Now go." The church that refuses belonging crushes its people. The church that refuses mission coddles its people. But the church that embraces both becomes the unstoppable force God designed.

This is why family must become an army. The Father is not content with children who never grow. He is calling sons and daughters to rise into maturity, to carry responsibility, to endure hardness, to march as soldiers of the cross.

Conclusion: From Audience to Army

The destiny of the church is not to remain a nursery, nor to remain a crowd. Its destiny is to be a family that becomes an army. Audiences will come and go, but families endure. Armies advance.

God is not gathering spectators. He is raising soldiers. He is calling His people to grow from milk to meat, from infancy to maturity, from dependency to dominion. The local church is where this transformation takes place, where believers are raised, trained, and sent.

As Paul declared: *"For the weapons of our warfare are not carnal, but mighty through God to the pulling down of strong holds"* (2 Corinthians 10:4). The battle is raging. The call is clear. The Spirit is summoning the church to rise, not as an audience, but as a family forged into an army.

The trumpet is sounding. The household of faith must answer. The only question left is this: will we remain consumers, or will we take our place as the army of the living God?

Scripture Index

Chapter Three

Abraham's 318 – Raising Trained Servants for Battle

Introduction

There is a reason the Spirit keeps pointing us back to Abraham's story. Abraham was not only the father of faith; he was the father of a household. He was not merely chosen to believe God but to raise a people who would carry covenant into battle. When Lot was taken captive, Abraham did not hire mercenaries from the nations. He turned to his own house. Out of his family he summoned three hundred and eighteen trained servants - men born in his house, loyal to his covenant, sharpened by discipline, and ready for war (Genesis 14:14).

This is the pattern for the Kingdom. God is not looking for borrowed strength, flashy numbers, or mercenary alliances. He is raising a people from within His house, sons and daughters who have been trained, disciplined, and made ready. Victory in the Kingdom does not belong to those who are naturally strong but to those who are spiritually prepared.

The Spirit declares again: God does not win battles through borrowed soldiers. He wins battles through trained sons.

Born in the House

Scripture makes a point to say Abraham's 318 were born in his house. They were not outsiders Abraham recruited when trouble came. They were not visitors passing through. They belonged to him. They carried his culture. They lived under his authority. They bore his discipline.

This is the difference between a crowd and a covenant family. A crowd can be gathered quickly, but when the enemy attacks, they scatter. Only those who are born in the house will remain when the battle comes. You cannot fight with people who do not share your covenant.

This is why the local church must raise sons and daughters, not just attract attenders. Borrowed strength will abandon you when the fight gets hard. Imported leaders will falter when loyalty is tested. But sons and daughters of the house - those who have been nurtured, trained, and disciplined - will stand shoulder to shoulder when the war horn sounds.

An audience applauds; an army obeys. A mercenary flees; a son remains.

Training vs. Natural Strength

Abraham's servants were not mighty warriors by natural birth. They were household men, trained under his leadership. Yet they overcame kings. How? Because victory does not come through natural strength but through trained obedience.

Paul told Timothy, *"Exercise thyself rather unto godliness. For bodily exercise profiteth little: but godliness is profitable unto all things"* (1 Timothy 4:7–8). Training in godliness produces soldiers who can endure hardship, resist temptation, and march in unity.

The Spirit is clear: Natural talent may impress, but only trained obedience wins battles. A worship team may sound skilled, but without discipline and unity, they are powerless in the spirit. A preacher may be eloquent, but without submission to God's Word, he is a sounding brass and a tinkling cymbal.

Training builds endurance. Training produces resilience. Training transforms weakness into strength. As scripture says, *"Blessed be the Lord my strength, which teacheth my hands to war, and my fingers to fight"* (Psalm 144:1). It is God Himself who trains His servants, and He does it within the household of faith.

The Discipline of Obedience

Abraham's household was marked not only by training but by obedience. When he called, they came. When he armed them, they received their weapons. When he marched, they followed. There was no debate, no delay, no division.

Victory comes not from numbers, but from unity and obedience. This is the unshakable principle of spiritual warfare. Gideon's army proved it. Three hundred men obeying God's strategy defeated multitudes of Midianites (Judges 7). Numbers are irrelevant when obedience is complete.

Jesus Himself modeled this. He did not gather a crowd to shake the world; He raised twelve men. Trained, tested, disciplined men who became the foundation of the church. *"And he ordained twelve, that they should be with him, and that he might send them forth to preach"* (Mark 3:14). He did not need thousands; He needed trained disciples.

So it is today. The modern church often chases numbers, thinking influence equals impact. But God is not impressed with attendance. He is moved by obedience. One obedient servant is more powerful than a thousand passive hearers.

Servants Who Become Soldiers

It is significant that Abraham's men are called "servants." They did not begin as soldiers; they began as servants. This is the pathway of the Kingdom. Before God makes a man a warrior, He makes him a servant. Before He grants authority, He requires submission.

Jesus declared, *"Whosoever will be great among you, let him be your minister; and whosoever will be chief among you, let him be your servant"* (Matthew 20:26–27). Soldiers in God's army are forged in the fire of servanthood. They learn humility before authority. They learn submission before command.

This is why many ministries collapse - they want warriors without servants, leaders without submission, soldiers without discipline. But true Kingdom order raises servants who become soldiers, sons who become leaders, disciples who become apostles.

The Danger of Borrowed Armor

When David prepared to face Goliath, Saul tried to clothe him in his own armor. But David refused. *"I cannot go with these; for I have not proved them"* (1 Samuel 17:39). Victory cannot be won with borrowed armor. You must fight with what you have been trained in.

In the same way, churches cannot win battles with borrowed strategies, imported systems, or man-made programs. The army God raises must fight with what they have proven in the house. Abraham's 318 did not need the weapons of foreign kings; they used what had been forged in their training.

Borrowed soldiers, borrowed armor, borrowed strategies - these all fail in the day of battle. Only trained servants born in the house, armed with weapons they have proven, can secure victory.

Raising Generations of Trained Servants

Abraham's 318 are not just a story; they are a prophetic picture of what the church must produce. Every local church is called to raise trained servants - sons and daughters who are loyal, disciplined, and ready to fight for the Kingdom.

This is why discipleship is so urgent. It is not about filling pews but forging warriors. It is not about programs but preparation. Every believer must be trained to pray with power, to wield the Word with accuracy, to walk in holiness, and to resist the schemes of the enemy.

The household of faith cannot be content with shallow believers who attend but never grow. We must raise a people who are ready for war, who understand spiritual authority, who are equipped with the armor of God (Ephesians 6:10–18).

Unity in the House

Abraham's servants did not fight as individuals; they fought as one. This is the essence of the Kingdom army: many members, one body (1 Corinthians 12:12). Division is the enemy's greatest weapon, but unity is heaven's unstoppable force.

Psalm 133 declares, *"Behold, how good and how pleasant it is for brethren to dwell together in unity… for there the Lord commanded the blessing"* (Psalm 133:1,3). Unity is not optional; it is essential. Without unity, there is no blessing. Without unity, there is no victory.

The church must therefore guard against comparison, competition, and jealousy. Soldiers who compare themselves with each other break rank. Servants who resent correction sabotage the house. Only a unified household can fight as Abraham's 318 did - with one heart, one mission, one covenant.

Conclusion: The Pattern for Victory

47

The story of Abraham's 318 is not a relic of history; it is a prophetic blueprint. God is not looking for mercenaries; He is raising sons. He is not impressed with crowds; He is training armies. He is not searching for borrowed strength; He is forging obedience in His house.

The principle is clear: victory belongs to those who are trained, loyal, obedient, and unified. It belongs to servants who have become soldiers, sons who have been disciplined, believers who have been raised in the house.

Abraham's household overcame kings because they were prepared. So too will the church overcome the powers of darkness when we raise trained servants in the house of God.

The trumpet is sounding. The call is urgent. The Lord is asking: will we remain audiences, or will we raise armies? Will we borrow strength, or will we train sons? Will we chase numbers, or will we build covenant families who can stand in battle?

The Spirit's answer is resounding: Raise the 318. Train the household. Prepare the army. For the day of battle is here.

Scripture Index

- Ephesians 6:10–18
- 1 Corinthians 12:12
- Psalm 133:1–3

Chapter Four

Spiritual Fathers and Mothers – Multiplying Healthy Generations

Introduction

Every great move of God is marked not just by revelation but by relationship. The Kingdom is never sustained by gifted instructors alone; it is carried forward by fathers and mothers who raise sons and daughters. The apostle Paul made it plain: *"For though ye have ten thousand instructors in Christ, yet have ye not many fathers"* (1 Corinthians 4:15).

Instructors can fill heads with knowledge, but only fathers and mothers can impart identity, discipline, and destiny. An instructor may explain principles, but a father reveals inheritance. A mother carries life and nourishes it until maturity is formed.

The local church is not merely an institution of teaching; it is a household of generations. Just as Abraham was chosen to command his household after him, so the church must raise up spiritual generations who will carry the covenant flame forward. We are not called to clone personalities or copy ministries, but to multiply health - to see sons and daughters grow into fathers and mothers who will then raise the next generation.

This is the divine cycle of multiplication: fathers and mothers raising sons and daughters, who then become fathers and mothers, until the Kingdom spans generations.

Not Many Fathers

Paul's words to the Corinthians are piercing: *"For though ye have ten thousand instructors in Christ, yet have ye not many fathers"* (1 Corinthians 4:15). Instruction is plentiful. Preaching is abundant. Seminars and teachings overflow. But fatherhood and motherhood are rare.

Why? Because fathers and mothers bear weight that instructors do not. An instructor can walk away after the lesson. A father cannot. An instructor may be applauded for eloquence. A mother sacrifices in secret, unseen by crowds. Fatherhood is costly. Motherhood demands selflessness.

You can have a thousand voices speak into your life, but it only takes one father to shape your destiny.

Instruction informs, but fatherhood transforms. Instruction can point the way, but fatherhood imparts courage to walk it. Sons and daughters may learn from instructors, but they are formed under fathers and mothers. This is why the church must rise beyond programs and step into parenting.

The Counterfeit of One Father

In every generation, the enemy tries to twist God's design. One of the distortions is the idea that believers can only have "one father." This false teaching attempts to limit spiritual relationship and breeds control, manipulation, and immaturity.

The Kingdom was never designed to orbit one man; it was designed to multiply generations. Fathers and mothers are not called to compete but to complement. Sons and daughters can draw from many streams of fatherhood and motherhood without being bound to idolatry of personality.

Paul called Timothy his son in the faith (1 Timothy 1:2), but he also called Titus his son (Titus 1:4). Elisha clung to Elijah, but he was also sharpened in the school of prophets. Even Jesus Himself submitted to Joseph as a boy, yet He also honored the ministry of John the Baptist as His forerunner.

Spiritual parenting is not about control; it is about release. True fathers and mothers do not monopolize; they multiply. They do not chain sons and daughters to themselves; they launch them into their own assignments.

Control produces clones, but covenant produces sons.

Sons and Daughters, Not Orphans

One of the greatest crises in the church today is the orphan spirit. Many believers have instructors but no fathers. They are filled with knowledge but empty of identity. They are gifted but

52

insecure. They are active in ministry but unrooted in covenant love.

The prophetic promise is this: *"And he shall turn the heart of the fathers to the children, and the heart of the children to their fathers"* (Malachi 4:6). When the orphan spirit is broken, hearts are healed, and generational blessing is released.

An orphan craves applause, but a son is secure in his father's approval. An orphan competes for attention, but a daughter rests in her mother's embrace. Orphans live with suspicion, but sons walk in trust.

Sons and daughters thrive in the presence of fathers and mothers. They learn how to endure correction without shame, how to walk in authority without arrogance, how to be faithful in little before being entrusted with much. They are sharpened like arrows in the hand of a warrior (Psalm 127:4).

Orphans multiply confusion; sons multiply stability.

And just as arrows are not meant to remain in the quiver, sons and daughters are not meant to stay hidden forever. They are meant to be released into battle, launched into assignment, carrying the heart of the house that raised them.

Seasons of Growth

Just as natural children pass through stages of development, so spiritual sons and daughters move through seasons of growth. Infants need nurture. Children need instruction. Adolescents need correction. Sons and daughters need responsibility. Fathers and mothers guide each stage with wisdom.

Paul modeled this with Timothy. At first, he was a young disciple, following Paul and learning from his example. Later, he was entrusted with leading churches, carrying the authority of his father in the faith. Eventually, Timothy himself became a father, discipling others in turn.

Growth requires patience. A father does not expect his toddler to run marathons. A mother does not demand her infant to feed itself. Each stage requires unique attention, unique correction, and unique encouragement.

Infants need milk, but sons need correction. Without correction, immaturity becomes rebellion. Without patience, correction becomes abuse.

Spiritual fathers and mothers know when to comfort and when to confront. They understand that growth is not instant - it is forged in seasons, through victories and failures, joys and tears.

Multiplication, Not Hoarding

The mark of true fatherhood and motherhood is multiplication. Insecure leaders hoard sons and daughters to themselves, afraid of losing influence. True fathers and mothers know their success is not measured by how many cling to them but by how many are released.

Paul commanded Timothy: *"The things that thou hast heard of me among many witnesses, the same commit thou to faithful men, who shall be able to teach others also"* (2 Timothy 2:2). This is four generations in one verse: Paul to Timothy, Timothy to faithful men, faithful men to others also. This is Kingdom multiplication.

True fathers don't compete with their sons; they commission them. True mothers don't resent their daughters; they release them. Leaders who hoard will see their legacy die with them. Fathers and mothers who multiply will see their legacy echo through generations.

Legacy is not measured by followers but by fruit.

The Heart of Fathers and Mothers

At the core of fatherhood and motherhood is love. Paul wrote to the Thessalonians, *"We were gentle among you, even as a nurse cherisheth her children... ye know how we exhorted and comforted and charged every one of you, as a father doth his children"* (1 Thessalonians 2:7,11).

Gentleness and exhortation, comfort and charge - this is the balance of parenting. Fathers and mothers carry tenderness and toughness. They embrace sons when they fall but also correct them when they err. They do not abandon in weakness, nor do they excuse rebellion. They love enough to discipline, and they discipline because they love.

Love without correction is sentimentality; correction without love is cruelty. Fatherhood requires both.

This is the heart of God Himself. *"Like as a father pitieth his children, so the Lord pitieth them that fear him"* (Psalm 103:13). When fathers and mothers reflect this heart, they reveal the nature of the heavenly Father to their sons and daughters.

Generational Legacy

The ultimate goal of fatherhood and motherhood is not comfort but legacy. Scripture declares, *"We will not hide them from their children, shewing to the generation to come the praises of the Lord, and his strength, and his wonderful works that he hath done"* (Psalm 78:4).

Every generation must raise the next. Abraham raised Isaac. Isaac raised Jacob. Jacob raised the twelve tribes. David raised Solomon. Paul raised Timothy. Jesus raised disciples who became apostles. The Kingdom advances through generational legacy.

When fathers stop raising sons, the Kingdom stops advancing.

Fathers and mothers who fail to raise sons and daughters create a gap that the enemy fills with orphans. But when generations are raised, multiplied, and released, the Kingdom expands exponentially.

Orphans multiply confusion. Fathers and mothers multiply health. Sons and daughters multiply legacy.

Conclusion: Multiplying Healthy Generations

The cry of this hour is not for more instructors. It is for fathers and mothers. It is for men and women who will carry the weight of covenant, the patience of love, and the courage of discipline. It is for leaders who will see beyond their own lifetime, beyond their own ministry, beyond their own recognition, and invest in the next generation.

Spiritual fatherhood and motherhood is not about titles. It is about tears, about sleepless nights, about sacrifices made in secret. It is about walking with sons and daughters until they stand on their own. It is about multiplying healthy generations until the Kingdom fills the earth.

The Lord is turning the hearts of fathers to children and the hearts of children to fathers. The orphan spirit is being broken. Sons and daughters are rising. And they, too, will become fathers and mothers.

The question remains: will we settle for instructors, or will we rise as fathers and mothers? Will we hoard followers, or will we multiply sons? Will we seek applause, or will we build legacy?

The Spirit is calling. The generations are waiting. It is time to multiply healthy generations.

Scripture Index

- 1 Corinthians 4:15
- 1 Timothy 1:2
- Titus 1:4
- Malachi 4:6
- Psalm 127:4–5

- 2 Timothy 2:2
- 1 Thessalonians 2:7
- 1 Thessalonians 2:11
- Psalm 103:13
- Psalm 78:4

Chapter Five

Bishops, Elders, and Deacons – Nature and Function in the New Testament Church

Introduction

The church of Jesus Christ is not sustained by charisma, popularity, or corporate strategy. It is held together by the divine order of God's Spirit. Leadership in the Kingdom is not a human invention; it is a heavenly design. The New Testament reveals three pillars of church function: elders, bishops, and deacons. These are not titles for the sake of honorific pride; they are functions for the sake of Kingdom health.

Paul wrote to the Philippians and addressed them *"with the bishops and deacons"* (Philippians 1:1), showing that even the earliest churches, some of them quite small, carried these essential roles. Without them, the house of God crumbles into confusion. With them, the house of God grows into a dwelling place for His glory.

This chapter is a call to rediscover the nature and function of biblical leadership. For without fathers and mothers, without trained servants, without appointed leaders who embody maturity and servanthood, the church loses its shape and forfeits its authority.

Elders: The Nature of Maturity

The word "elder" does not describe an office so much as it describes a nature. An elder is not made by election; he is revealed by maturity. Eldership is the fruit of years, of scars, of seasons walked faithfully with God.

Peter exhorted the elders, *"Feed the flock of God which is among you, taking the oversight thereof, not by constraint, but willingly; not for filthy lucre, but of a ready mind"* (1 Peter 5:2). Elders are not dictators but shepherds. Their authority is not rooted in force but in faithfulness.

An elder is not made by a vote; he is proven by seasons. Elders emerge because the Spirit of God has tested them, pruned them, and established them.

Elders are not promoted, they are revealed. A true elder cannot be manufactured by men's councils. His maturity is proven in storms, his wisdom forged in fire, his steadiness confirmed by years of faithfulness.

Paul told Timothy, *"Let the elders that rule well be counted worthy of double honour, especially they who labour in the word and doctrine"* (1 Timothy 5:17). Elders do not chase honor; they earn it by consistency. Their very lives preach a sermon of endurance.

Elders embody stability. They are anchors in the house of God. Their very presence speaks of faithfulness.

Bishops: The Function of Oversight

If elder describes a nature, bishop describes a function. The Greek word episkopos means overseer, one who watches over, guards, and governs. A bishop is not a different class of leader but an elder entrusted with oversight.

Paul declared, *"This is a true saying, If a man desire the office of a bishop, he desireth a good work"* (1 Timothy 3:1). Notice carefully - he desires not a crown, but a work. Bishop is not a title of rank but a weight of responsibility.

The work defines the man. Elder is the nature; bishop is the function. Oversight requires vision, discernment, and courage. It requires the ability to see wolves before they devour the sheep, to recognize false doctrine before it spreads, to govern with a father's heart rather than a tyrant's hand.

Oversight is not a crown; it is a cross. In the Kingdom, authority always bends lower in service. The greater the call to oversight, the deeper the call to humility. Servant-leadership is not weakness; it is the pattern of Christ, the Chief Shepherd who stooped to wash feet. The bishop carries burdens no one else sees, prays prayers no one else hears, and fights battles no one else knows.

Bishops are not CEOs. They are shepherd-overseers. Their calling is to guide, to guard, to govern, and to grow the people of God. They carry responsibility, not prestige. To bear the function of bishop is to stand watch in the night, to carry the burden of intercession, to ensure the house of God remains aligned to the cornerstone.

Deacons: Servant Leadership

If bishops govern and elders embody maturity, deacons reveal the heart of servant leadership. The very word diakonos means servant. Deacons are not junior executives; they are frontline servants who embody the humility of Christ.

When a dispute arose in the early church over the daily distribution of food, the apostles appointed deacons to handle the matter so they could continue in prayer and the ministry of the Word (Acts 6:1–4). Deacons were not appointed because they were talented administrators but because they were full of the Holy Ghost and wisdom.

If you cannot serve tables, you cannot serve the Kingdom. Those who despise service disqualify themselves from true leadership.

This is the divine paradox: those who serve tables with integrity carry heaven's authority. In the Kingdom, servanthood is not the pathway to leadership - it is leadership.

Paul greeted the church at Philippi *"with the bishops and deacons"* (Philippians 1:1), showing that deacons are not secondary but essential. Without deacons, the practical life of the church collapses. Without their hands, the ministry of the Word becomes hindered. Deacons are the lifeblood of service, embodying Christ who came not to be served but to serve.

Deacons are the hands that carry the vision when the weight is too much for one man. They embody the truth that Kingdom leadership is always measured by how well you serve.

Distinctions Without Division

Elder, bishop, and deacon are distinct, but they are not divided. They work in harmony, each carrying a unique weight for the health of the body.

- Elder = nature. Elders reveal maturity, the seasoned life that becomes an anchor.

- Bishop = function. Bishops carry oversight, watching, guarding, and governing.

- Deacon = service. Deacons carry humility, serving the house and embodying the gospel through action.

Confusion comes when nature, function, and service are replaced with ambition, position, and performance. When men chase titles instead of transformation, the order of God is corrupted.

But when the distinctions are held rightly, the church flourishes. Elders steady, bishops oversee, deacons serve. Together they form a leadership fabric that cannot easily be torn.

Qualifications and Integrity

Paul laid out qualifications for bishops and deacons in 1 Timothy 3 and Titus 1. These qualifications are not about charisma but about character. They are not about gifting but about integrity.

"A bishop then must be blameless, the husband of one wife, vigilant, sober, of good behaviour, given to hospitality, apt to teach; not given to wine, no striker, not greedy of filthy lucre; but patient, not a brawler, not covetous" (1 Timothy 3:2–3).

"Likewise must the deacons be grave, not doubletongued, not given to much wine, not greedy of filthy lucre; holding the mystery of the faith in a pure conscience" (1 Timothy 3:8–9).

Titles without testimony are nothing but religious costumes. The badge of honor in the Kingdom is not a title but a life that bears fruit.

Paul emphasized family: *"For if a man know not how to rule his own house, how shall he take care of the church of God?"* (1 Timothy 3:5).

The first pulpit you must master is your own home. If you cannot shepherd your spouse and children, you cannot shepherd God's people.

Character is the currency of Kingdom leadership. A man may preach with power, but if his house is in disarray, he is disqualified. A woman may serve with zeal, but if her integrity is corrupt, her service is void.

Authority without integrity is rebellion. Leadership without character is fraud.

Why This Matters for Today

Why does all this matter? Because when the church abandons God's order, chaos follows. When elders are ignored, wisdom is lost. When bishops are idolized, oversight becomes tyranny. When deacons are dismissed, service collapses.

When churches build like corporations, they collapse like corporations. When they build like Kingdom, they endure like a Kingdom.

Many churches today have embraced worldly models of leadership - pastors as CEOs, elders as board members, deacons as errand runners. But this is not the Kingdom. The Kingdom does not copy corporations; it embodies covenant.

God's house is healthiest when its leaders embody His order. Elders anchor, bishops oversee, deacons serve. Together they reveal Christ, the Chief Shepherd, the ultimate Overseer, the Servant of all.

When the church returns to this blueprint, it becomes unshakable. Elders carry the testimony of seasons. Bishops carry the vision of oversight. Deacons carry the towel of service. And together, the house of God stands in strength.

Conclusion: God's Blueprint for Leadership

The church is not built on titles; it is built on lives laid down. Elders, bishops, and deacons are not ranks of status but functions of service. They exist not to lord over the flock but to lay down their lives for it.

This is God's blueprint for leadership: maturity, oversight, and service woven together. Elders reveal the wisdom of age. Bishops carry the responsibility of oversight. Deacons embody the humility of service. Each is essential. None can be discarded.

The church does not need celebrities; it needs elders. The church does not need executives; it needs bishops. The church does not need volunteers; it needs deacons. The church does not need titles; it needs testimony.

This is not optional. Without this order, the church falls into confusion. With it, the church advances in strength.

The blueprint has been given. The call is clear. The time is now.

Scripture Index

Chapter Six

Beginning the Process of Identifying Leaders

Introduction: Leadership That Multiplies Beyond Twelve

Leadership is not born out of theory - it is born out of obedience. Every generation must rediscover heaven's design for raising leaders that multiply the Kingdom beyond themselves. Yet today, a subtle deception has crept into the church, cloaked in academic reasoning called "spiritual formation and G-12" programs: the belief that people cannot effectively train more than twelve people because Jesus only had twelve disciples.

That teaching sounds humble, but it is wrong. It is not scriptural - it is psychological, born from secular misreadings of group theory rather than divine pattern. Jesus never limited His leadership to twelve; He multiplied His reach through layers of disciples. Scripture says He *appointed seventy others also, and sent them two by two before His face into every city and place, whither He Himself would come* (Luke 10:1). Later, *about one hundred and twenty* gathered in the upper room (Acts 1:15). And before the cross, *great multitudes followed Him from Galilee, Decapolis, Jerusalem, Judea, and beyond Jordan* (Matthew 4:25).

Jesus knew how to disciple twelve, mobilize seventy, and lead multitudes. The Son of God did not limit leadership; He expanded it through structure, alignment, and anointing. When men impose ceilings that God never established, they shrink the Kingdom to the size of their fears.

Leadership in the Kingdom is scalable because grace is not a scarce resource. God told Moses to appoint *"rulers of thousands, hundreds, fifties, and tens"* (Exodus 18:21). Each man was promoted according to capacity. The same principle governs the modern church.

The Fallacy of the "Twelve" and the Limits of Secular Thinking

The idea that a leader can only guide twelve people originates not from Scripture, but from the misapplication of *Dunbar's Number* and other sociological theories about group cohesion. Those models may work in classrooms or corporations that operate without the Spirit - but the Church is not built on human bandwidth; it is built on divine order.

Leadership researchers like **Tuckman (1965)** and **Hersey & Blanchard (1977)** demonstrated that effective leadership depends not on group size but on clarity, communication, and the maturity of those being led. The same truth appears in the Word of God.

Jesus had an inner circle of three (Peter, James, John), a core of twelve, an extended circle of seventy, and multitudes who followed His teaching. These were concentric layers of influence, not limitations of capacity. Kingdom leadership expands according to obedience, not psychology.

Spiritual Formation and the Kingdom Blueprint

The phrase spiritual formation did not begin with Renovaré. It existed long before the movement attempted to redefine it. Historically, the term referred simply to the shaping of the believer's inner life by the Spirit of God through obedience to Christ and participation in the life of His Church. Yet, in the modern era, its meaning has been clouded by competing philosophies and by movements that merge streams never meant to flow together.

Renovaré - founded by author Richard Foster - describes itself as "Christian in commitment, ecumenical in breadth, international in scope." (Wikipedia, "Renovaré"). It defines spiritual formation as "the process by which Christ-likeness is established in the depths of our being." (Renovaré.org). On the surface this sounds noble, yet its foundation is intentionally broad. Renovaré teaches from six "streams" of Christian tradition— Contemplative, Holiness, Charismatic, Social Justice, Evangelical, and Incarnational - drawing from Catholic, Protestant, and other influences in an attempt to unify them into one expression of devotion.

The issue is not the desire for holiness but the mixture of sources that results. Some of the contemplative practices Renovaré promotes - silence, solitude, meditation, and inward focus—are similar in form to Buddhist disciplines, though different in stated purpose. One account observes, "His interest in contemplation led him to investigate prayer-forms in Eastern religion... Zen masters from Asia regarded him as the preeminent authority on their kind of prayer in the United States." (Cited in Christian Forums, "The Spiritual Formation, Renovaré, Richard Foster and the Emerging Church Movement").

While Renovaré does not officially teach Buddhist doctrine, critics note that its openness to Eastern contemplative methods, Catholic mysticism, and ecumenical synthesis blurs doctrinal clarity. A report from ReachOut Trust explains that Renovaré's model "blends Catholic, Protestant, and even non-Christian mystical practices in a way that may weaken doctrinal boundaries." (ReachOutTrust.org). Other researchers, such as Lighthouse Trails, warn that the same mysticism which once separated monastic devotion from biblical discipleship has re-entered the modern church through Renovaré's vocabulary of formation.

Renovaré does not claim that Catholicism and Protestantism are identical in doctrine, yet its practical ecumenism gives extraordinary room to mystics, contemplatives, and non-Protestant figures without clear qualification. The result is a system that sounds biblical but functions by borrowed spirituality - a house built with materials from many kingdoms.

The Kingdom Definition

In the Kingdom, spiritual formation is not found in blended mysticism or imported meditation. It is the biblical process of discipleship through covenant relationship - the training of believers within the family of God until sons and daughters mature into fathers and mothers in the faith. It is not the shaping of the soul by introspection but the transformation of the heart by obedience.

True formation is not learned through contemplative silence but through the fire of relationship, correction, and submission to the Spirit within the household of faith. It cannot be franchised by program or number. Jesus did not institutionalize twelve followers; He imparted His life until they bore His nature. The Church is not a monastery of quiet seekers but a family of trained builders - sons and daughters who rise as fathers and mothers, governed not by ecumenical trends but by the Word of the King.

Therefore, in the language of this book and of Kingdom educators, spiritual formation means biblical discipleship through covenant relationships - training believers within the local church until maturity is formed and generational multiplication begins. We do not structure by number; we structure by relationship and obedience to the Spirit. For in the Kingdom, transformation does not flow from silence or solitude, but from surrender and service.

True spiritual formation is not the philosophical revision introduced by Dallas Willard, Richard Foster, or the Renovaré Institute, but the ancient Kingdom pattern of discipleship rooted in covenant relationship and obedience to the Spirit.

Kingdom Discipleship vs. Spiritual Formation (attempted redefine by Renovaré Model) and G12 Models

The Kingdom does not advance through formulas or modern philosophies of "spiritual formation." It advances through fathers and mothers who raise sons and daughters in covenant. What many call *spiritual formation* often replaces the fire of obedience with the theory of self-improvement. It speaks of reflection more than repentance and produces students rather than soldiers. The New Testament Church did not grow through contemplative systems or controlled networks; it multiplied through relationship, obedience, and the power of the Holy Spirit.

Likewise, the "G12" pattern of organizing believers into groups of twelve may have borrowed language from Jesus' ministry, but it misses His method. Jesus did not build a pyramid of performance; He built a family of obedience. The strength of His twelve was not in the number but in the proximity - men who walked with Him, ate with Him, and watched His life until His nature became their own. True discipleship is not numerical but relational. It cannot be franchised or charted on a spreadsheet. It is birthed in the altar of relationship and matured in the furnace of obedience.

Kingdom discipleship, therefore, is not spiritual formation by theory, nor is it a group model by design. It is the training of sons and daughters in the household of faith - where believers are corrected, tested, and equipped until the nature of Christ is seen in them. It is a living apprenticeship under fathers and mothers who carry the heart of God. In this, every local church becomes a family that becomes an army - not through programs, but through presence; not through counting people, but through reproducing character.

The Academic Gospel That Lost Its Fire

The work promoted by Dallas Willard, Richard Foster, and the Renovaré Institute was never fully embraced by the Church. Many pastors and congregations found it lifeless - intellectual rather than transformational, reflective rather than redemptive. The complaint was simple: *it was not biblical, and it was painfully dull to hear.* When the local church rejected it, academia adopted it. Seminaries began teaching what the sanctuary refused to receive, dressing the absence of power in the language of philosophy. And from those classrooms, a generation of ministers emerged fluent in theory but starved of fire.

Churches that later imported this academic model discovered the same outcome - still no power, still no growth, still the same fatigue of listening without transformation. The classroom cannot manufacture revival; it can only analyze what once burned. Academic influence has not healed the problem; it has magnified it. (Tuckman, 1965)

Prophetic insight:

When the *Gospel of the Kingdom* is preached in truth and power, it always works. It is never boring. It multiplies. It delivers. It transforms. But when men preach a diluted gospel, or preach it outside of Kingdom order, it will never produce fruit. The problem is not with the Gospel - it is with how it is being preached. The real Gospel carries the fire of heaven; the counterfeit only carries the echo of a lecture hall.

Leadership Is Proven Through Multiplication

I have led many groups, built many teams, and managed organizations ranging from a handful to thousands. The truth is consistent across every scale: leadership is discovered through observation and multiplied through opportunity.

When I first became the pastor of a teen group many years ago, in a small church, the church had no youth at all. Within twelve weeks, that changed. The group grew to more than forty-five teenagers, and in a few months, more than the adult congregation. Leadership always manifests through fruitfulness. *By their fruits you shall know them* (Matthew 7:20).

My process for identifying leaders was intentional. I gave everyone a chance to build something of their own - a voluntary project, a team, or an event. Then I observed how they built it. Did they rally people? Did they solve conflict or create it? Did they complete the task with excellence or chaos?

Those who could gather and maintain unity without drama revealed a leadership gift. Those who constantly generated conflict or manipulated others exposed immaturity or selfish ambition. Leadership is not about what you build - it is about how you build.

The Spiritual Principle of Alignment: The Oil Flows Down

Psalm 133 paints the picture of divine order and spiritual transfer: *"It is like the precious oil upon the head, running down upon the beard, even Aaron's beard, that went down to the skirts of his garments."*

The oil runs down - it never runs up. When God anoints a leader, that anointing flows to those aligned under proper authority. It is impossible to serve faithfully under true anointing and not receive overflow. The closer you stand to the altar, the more oil touches your life.

This is the secret of leadership development. If you get close to those who handle oil and sacrifice - those who labor in prayer, carry the burden of the altar, and serve with pure motives - the same anointing that rests upon them begins to rest upon you.

But this principle carries a warning. Just as oil flows down, so does corruption. If you place someone in leadership out of anger, retaliation, or favoritism, their spirit flows into the people they lead. If the "junk" in them is unhealed, it spreads like infection through the body. This is why Paul warned, *"Lay hands suddenly on no man, neither be partaker of other men's sins: keep thyself pure"* (1 Timothy 5:22).

Leadership appointment is sacred. You do not place people to punish others. You place people because they carry oil. What flows from the head defines the health of the whole body.

When God Promotes to Punish

There is another sobering truth rarely preached today: sometimes God promotes a person not to bless them, but to expose and judge them. Promotion can either lift you or reveal the problems in an organization..

King Saul was *anointed with oil and made king* at the people's demand (1 Samuel 10:1, 1 Samuel 8:7). Yet his promotion was a form of divine discipline. Israel rejected God's direct rule, so He allowed Saul to rise - *"that they may see what their desire brings."* Saul's leadership exposed the nation's rebellion and brought correction through its consequence.

Likewise, Pharaoh was *raised up* not as a vessel of mercy but as a vessel of demonstration. God said, *"For this very purpose have I raised thee up, to show in thee My power, and that My name may be declared throughout all the earth"* (Exodus 9:16, Romans 9:17). Pharaoh's promotion was not exaltation - it was exposure.

There are seasons when heaven promotes a man, not to bless, but to expose. Divine elevation can arrive as either a reward or a correction, even to a ministry.

Elisha once traveled to Damascus while Ben-hadad, king of Syria, lay sick. The king sent his trusted servant Hazael with forty camel-loads of gifts to inquire of the prophet, *"Shall I recover of this disease?"* (2 Kings 8:7–9). Elisha looked through the question and into the soul of the messenger. *"Go, say unto him, Thou mayest certainly recover: howbeit the Lord hath shewed me that he shall surely die."* Then the prophet fixed his gaze upon Hazael until the man was ashamed - and Elisha wept.

When Hazael asked why, the prophet answered, "Because I know the evil that thou wilt do unto the children of Israel." Elisha saw a crown in the shadows and blood on the throne. He knew that this servant, once trusted, would soon rise through treachery. The next day Hazael suffocated his king with a wet cloth and seized the throne. What looked like promotion was really judgment. God permitted the ascent of a man whose ambition would scourge a nation—because Israel had rejected correction.

Prophetic Insight:

Sometimes the Lord promotes a leader not to reward obedience but to discipline rebellion (sin) beneath them. When the appointed voice refuses heaven's instruction and installs another out of fear, politics, or preference, divine order is broken. The wrong appointment opens the door for the wrong spirit. The oil that was meant to flow in blessing begins to flow in chastening.

Elisha's tears reveal the heart of God - He grieves even while He judges. Israel's disobedience birthed its own oppressor. Hazael's crown was a mirror held up to the nation's heart. In the same way, churches and leaders who reject divine alignment often find themselves ruled by the very spirit they entertained. God allows what they insisted upon, until repentance restores order.

The Principle:

Promotion without purity becomes punishment.

Elevation without obedience becomes exposure.

When God tells a man whom to choose and he chooses differently, destiny stalls. The anointing pauses. The flow of heaven waits until the misaligned vessel is removed. Leadership is not a game of preference - it is the stewardship of divine order. Heaven measures obedience, not popularity.

One word of caution in promotion: if the Lord told you to promote someone, do it. Don't test the person yourself to find out. You cannot duplicate the DNA God put in someone else. The punishment can be made worse, and now you include yourself in the correction due to disobedience and miss your destiny.

These examples remind us that **promotion without purity is punishment disguised as success**. When leaders rise without character, they often become instruments of judgment instead of blessing.

The Testing of the Builder's Heart

I used a system of progressive testing:

- **The Gathering Test:** Could they draw others through character and vision rather than manipulation?
- **The Harmony Test:** Did they bring unity or division?
- **The Execution Test:** Could they carry a task from vision to completion?
- **The Reaction Test:** How did they handle correction or delay?
- **The Spotlight Test:** Could they share credit and celebrate others?

The answers exposed not only skill but nature.

A person who must always be seen will eventually blind the team. Scripture says, *"Only by pride cometh contention"* (Proverbs 13:10). Pride divides; humility multiplies. A true leader learns to give others the stage while guarding the vision.

I also watched how other groups reacted to emerging leaders. Jealousy or sabotage from nearby teams often revealed more about those teams' leaders than the one being tested. If another group tried to undermine the new one, discipline was necessary - not just for the individuals but for the spirit that tolerated strife.

Some Are Called to Tens, Hundreds, and Thousands

As Moses' structure shows, leadership must align with grace. *"Moreover thou shalt provide out of all the people able men, such as fear God... and place such over them, to be rulers of thousands, and hundreds, and fifties, and tens"* (Exodus 18:21).

Not every leader is called to the same capacity. Some are called to shepherd ten; others, a thousand. The tragedy comes when we put someone called to tens over hundreds - the group will shrink. Conversely, putting one called to thousands over tens frustrates them and stagnates the ministry. Wisdom discerns scope.

The anointing defines the level of responsibility. If the oil on your life is for hundreds, then hundreds will follow. You do not need to force growth; you need to steward grace.

Guarding Against the Entertainer Spirit

In every organization, you will encounter "entertainer" personalities - charismatic, energetic, and magnetic. They attract crowds quickly, but if untrained, they also attract chaos. Their desire for attention breeds gossip, cliques, and spiritual confusion.

Before promoting such individuals, test them at the altar. Do they seek the spotlight or the sacrifice? If they crave applause, they will drain the oil. Leaders who serve from ego create atmospheres of competition instead of collaboration.

James warned, *"For where envying and strife is, there is confusion and every evil work"* (James 3:16). Until pride dies, promotion will destroy. The Lord does promote - but promotion can lift you up or expose you publicly if your character cannot carry the weight.

Development Through Proximity

Leadership cannot be developed in isolation. It is cultivated through proximity - walking beside those already carrying the oil. Elisha received Elijah's mantle not because he studied from afar, but because he *poured water on the hands of Elijah* (2 Kings 3:11). He served until the oil flowed down.

That is why the closer a person gets to true leadership - the ones who labor, sacrifice, and pray - the more the same grace begins to mark their life. Leadership is learned by serving under it. As the oil on Aaron's beard touched his garments, so the anointing on the leader transfers to those who dwell together in unity.

This is also why you must guard who you allow to lead. If the head is sick, the body suffers. If the leader's motives are corrupt, the infection spreads. The oil principle works both ways - it magnifies purity and multiplies impurity.

Practical Evaluation: Observation and Growth

Once potential leaders have been identified, let them lead established teams. Observe what happens. Does the group grow spiritually, relationally, and numerically - or does it fracture?

If a group under new leadership shrinks, investigate why. The issue may be personality, pride, or lack of structure. Leadership is not about perfection but about adaptability. As Paul said, *"Examine yourselves, whether ye be in the faith; prove your own selves"* (2 Corinthians 13:5).

Leadership development requires ongoing reflection, feedback, and correction. True leaders do not fear evaluation - they welcome it.

Blending Spiritual Wisdom and Practical Science

The principles of modern leadership theory confirm what Scripture already declared. Tuckman's research shows that effective teams must move through *forming, storming, norming, and performing*. Hersey and Blanchard's *Situational Leadership Model* teaches that leaders must adapt their style to the maturity of their followers. (Hersey & Blanchard, 1977)

Moses did the same when he delegated according to capacity. Jesus did it when He empowered the seventy. Paul did it when he trained Timothy and Titus differently according to their temperament and assignment.

Spiritual leadership is both prophetic and practical. It requires prayer *and* process, anointing *and* administration. The oil flows through structure, not chaos.

Leadership and the Birth Question

Are leaders born or made? The answer is yes - all people are born, but not all are developed. Some may have stronger natural gifts, but every gift must be refined. Even David - anointed as a boy - needed years of wilderness to become a king.

Leadership is not discovered in the spotlight; it is forged in obscurity. God develops leaders in hidden seasons where character is built and motives are purified.

Conclusion: Leadership as Legacy and Flow

Leadership in the Kingdom is both inheritance and responsibility. It is oil flowing downward, not ambition clawing upward. When the oil runs pure, the whole body flourishes. When it is polluted, the body suffers.

The modern church must rediscover this principle. You do not appoint to punish. You do not promote to prove a point. You elevate those whom the oil already marks.

The question is not how many you can lead - it is how faithfully you can steward the oil that flows through you. Whether you lead ten or ten thousand, your mandate is the same: multiply righteous leaders, guard the altar, and keep the flow pure.

For *"He gave some, apostles; some, prophets; some, evangelists, and some, pastors and teachers; for the perfecting of the saints, for the work of ministry, for the edifying of the body of Christ"* (Ephesians 4:11–12).

The oil must never stop flowing.

Scripture References

- Luke 10:1
- Acts 1:15
- Matthew 4:25
- Exodus 18:21
- Psalm 133:2
- Matthew 7:20
- 1 Timothy 5:22
- 1 Samuel 10:1
- 1 Samuel 8:7
- Exodus 9:16
- Romans 9:17
- Proverbs 13:10
- James 3:16
- 2 Kings 3:11
- 2 Corinthians 13:5
- Ephesians 4:11–12

Reference Sources

- Renovaré official website – https://renovare.org/about/ideas/spiritual-formation

- Wikipedia: "Renovaré." https://en.wikipedia.org/wiki/Renovar%C3%A9

- ReachOut Trust: "Richard Foster and Renovaré." https://reachouttrust.org/richard-foster-and-renovare

- Christian Forums Discussion: "The Spiritual Formation, Renovaré, Richard Foster and the Emerging Church Movement." https://www.christianforums.com

- Lighthouse Trails Research: "Renovaré Study Bible and Contemplative Influence." https://www.lighthousetrailsresearch.com/renovarestudybible.htm

Chapter Seven

When Rabbits Rule the Altar - The Sin Behind the Curtain

Introduction: Historical Prelude: The Fire and the Curtain

Before there was applause, there was obedience. Before there was a stage, there was an altar. In the days of Moses, the glory of God dwelled behind a curtain - a veil that only the high priest could pass once a year with blood for atonement (Leviticus 16:2). That veil symbolized separation between the Holy and the common. But when Christ gave up the ghost, *"the veil of the temple was rent in twain from the top to the bottom"* (Matthew 27:51). Heaven declared that no more would there be division between God and His people. Yet centuries later, the Church has sewn new curtains - made not of fabric, but of gossip, control, and performance. Leaders hide behind charisma. Congregations applaud personalities. The altar where the fire once fell has become a stage where actors perform. And just like in Ezekiel's vision, the Spirit still says, *"Son of man, dig into the wall"* (Ezekiel 8:7). For behind that curtain lies the sin that kills revival - hidden conversations, uncorrected immaturity, and private corruption masked by public holiness.

The Spirit of Gossip: Poison in the House

Gossip is the serpent that slithers between pews, whispering division into the hearts of believers. It is the venom of Hell disguised as discernment. Jesus gave the solution clearly: *"If thy brother shall trespass against thee, go and tell him his fault between thee and him alone"* (Matthew 18:15). But religious gossipers ignore that command. They prefer private audiences over holy confrontation. They perform prayer meetings that are really gossip rehearsals, retelling pain for attention rather than reconciliation. Paul warned, *"For I fear… debates, envyings, wraths, strifes, backbitings, whisperings, swellings, tumults"* (2 Corinthians 12:20). Gossipers are like spiritual rabbits in the dream - quick to multiply, fast to run, and impossible to catch once released. They hop from person to person, from text to text, spreading offense faster than truth can correct it. A leader who listens to gossip becomes addicted to it. It gives the illusion of power - the rush of control - but it is no different than pornography. Both are perversions of intimacy. Gossip creates a counterfeit sense of closeness, a false intimacy built on the nakedness of others.

When Leaders Enable Rabbits

Rabbits multiply faster than truth can chase them. When leaders refuse correction, they open the door for chaos to breed under their watch. Rabbits are not foxes - they are not predators - but their immaturity can ruin a vineyard all the same (Song of

Songs 2:15). They are emotional, impulsive, and easily offended. When the altar becomes a rabbit den, gossip becomes culture and division becomes normal. The immature spirit hides behind busyness. Rabbits always seem active - running from one ministry to another, one meeting to another - but movement is not maturity. The local church becomes a burrow of confusion, where untrained people chase roles instead of righteousness. Growth halts until someone stands in the authority of Christ and drives out the rabbits from the altar.

The Stage and the Curtain: The Theater of Religion

The church has become a theater where people perform instead of worship. The curtain that once separated the holy from the unholy has now become a prop - a cover for hypocrisy. Behind it, leaders rehearse holiness but live in compromise. They have traded the fire of conviction for the applause of the crowd. Jesus said, *"This people honoureth me with their lips, but their heart is far from me"* (Matthew 15:8). Behind every false revival is a curtain no one dared to pull back. Behind every scandal lies a script of ambition written in secrecy. What was meant to be a sanctuary has become a stage, and what should have been an altar has become a performance hall.

The Addiction to Information and Control

Information has become the drug of the modern pulpit. Leaders crave it - not revelation from heaven, but gossip from earth. They confuse surveillance with discernment. James warned, *"This wisdom descendeth not from above, but is earthly, sensual, devilish"* (James 3:15). When information becomes a means of control, it becomes witchcraft. Leaders who manipulate through what they know cease to be shepherds - they become stage directors controlling a cast of frightened actors. Such churches operate on fear, not faith. They do not raise disciples - they produce performers. Heaven calls it Babylon - a kingdom built on control, not covenant.

The False Fathers and the Spirit of Babylon

The Spirit of the Lord is exposing leaders who rule like bosses but not fathers. They sound like factory foremen from the 1920s - barking orders, demanding loyalty, dismissing people like disposable employees. They say to the saints, "I don't need you," or "You're replaceable," as though the Church were a business franchise. Paul declared, *"Though ye have ten thousand instructors in Christ, yet have ye not many fathers"* (1 Corinthians 4:15). True fathers do not say to their sons, "I don't want you." They may correct, but they never cast away. The boss mentality is not Kingdom - it is Babylon. It produces laborers, not sons; fear, not faith; compliance, not covenant. Even Fortune 500 corporations handle people better than many churches. Corporations have HR systems and accountability, while churches often excuse abuse under 'spiritual authority.' The Church should be the safest house on earth - not a stage of exploitation. The Kingdom is a family, governed by fathers and mothers who reflect the heart of God.

Immaturity on the Altar

Paul warned, *"Not a novice, lest being lifted up with pride he fall into the condemnation of the devil"* (1 Timothy 3:6). Yet many churches are run by novices - young leaders who mistake charisma for calling. They are zealous but untrained, energetic but unbroken. When 20-year-olds lead 20-year-olds without fathers above them, immaturity becomes policy. The church begins to reflect adolescence - high emotion, low endurance, and constant offense.

Family Idolatry and the Absalom Spirit

Behind many curtains of ministry is an idol shaped like family. Churches have turned into dynasties - pulpits passed down like thrones. This is the Absalom spirit - the smiling manipulator who flatters the people while plotting rebellion (2 Samuel 15:1–6). David refused to confront it, and the kingdom nearly collapsed. When family loyalty replaces Kingdom alignment, the Spirit departs. Favoritism destroys purity. *"He that ruleth his house well... for if a man know not how to rule his own house, how shall he take care of the church of God?"* (1 Timothy 3:4–5).

The Church Without Correction

When correction is rejected, the curtain grows thicker and the rabbits multiply. Churches that fear confrontation exalt rebellion in the name of grace. Leaders excuse compromise because they're afraid of losing tithers. Members resent discipline because they've confused it with condemnation. The Lord says, *"As many as I love, I rebuke and chasten"* (Revelation 3:19). A church without correction has already lost Christ.

Exposure: When God Pulls the Curtain

The Spirit of God will not sit silently while His sanctuary becomes a stage. *"For there is nothing covered, that shall not be revealed; neither hid, that shall not be known"* (Luke 12:2). God is pulling the curtain, exposing unholy alliances, hidden lusts, and manipulation. He is removing performers and restoring priests. When Nehemiah returned, he found Tobiah living in the temple storerooms and threw him out (Nehemiah 13:11). God is doing the same now - cleansing pulpits so His glory may return.

Restoring the Altar: Fathers, Not Bosses

Judgment begins at the house of God (1 Peter 4:17). But mercy begins with fathers who will rebuild what Babylon broke. The Spirit calls for leaders who rule not as foremen but as fathers. We need fathers who correct with compassion and leaders who model heaven's government - not the world's greed. When fathers rise, the family will heal. When the altar is cleansed, the fire will fall.

Prophetic Summary - When God Allows a Hazael

Sometimes when a church refuses correction, God does not immediately destroy it - He allows a Hazael to rise.

He permits an ambitious leader or immature voice to gain influence, not as a reward, but as a mirror. Just as Hazael ascended by deceit and became the rod of judgment against a rebellious people (2 Kings 8:7–15), so too God allows certain leaders to ascend when a house rejects His appointed order. Their rise exposes what the altar tried to hide.

When gossip replaces grace and charisma replaces character, Heaven withdraws its covering and allows chaos to discipline the proud. The people who demanded their own way receive it - and it devours them. These seasons are not without mercy; they are Heaven's last warning before cleansing fire falls.

Every stage built on rebellion eventually becomes a scaffold of exposure. God will let a Hazael rise until the hidden sin under the curtain is brought into the light. Then He tears the curtain, removes the pretenders, and restores true fathers to the altar.

Prophetic Insight:

When a people will not listen to correction, God sends them a mirror. When a leader refuses alignment, God raises a Hazael to reveal the heart of the house. Promotion without purity is punishment; exposure is Heaven's mercy before judgment.

The Spirit of the Lord says, "I am pulling down the stage built on rebellion and rebuilding the altar of repentance. I am exposing false crowns so the true oil may flow again.

The Trumpet Call: The Spirit Is Speaking

The Spirit of the Lord is saying: "I am tearing down the stage and rebuilding the altar. I am exposing what was done in the dark and bringing it into the light. The days of performance are ending, and the days of purity are beginning. I am raising fathers who love My people more than their platform. I am removing the boss spirit of Babylon and restoring the heart of the Father. I am silencing the rabbits and revealing the remnant. I am tearing the curtain so My glory may fill the house again. The stage will burn, but the altar will blaze with My fire."

So let the rabbits be cast out. Let the curtain fall. Let every hidden thing come to light. And let the builders of the Kingdom rise again - pure in heart, bold in truth, and filled with the fire of the Living God.

Scripture Index

Chapter Eight

The Power of Testimony – Overcoming by the Blood of the Lamb and the Word of Testimony

Introduction

The Kingdom of God does not advance by silence. It does not expand by hidden stories or sealed lips. It advances when the redeemed speak boldly of what the Lord has done. Revelation declares: *"And they overcame him by the blood of the Lamb, and by the word of their testimony; and they loved not their lives unto the death"* (Revelation 12:11).

This is heaven's blueprint for victory. The blood of the Lamb secures salvation. The word of testimony enforces it. Together they form a weapon no demon can withstand. The blood gives you victory, but your testimony enforces it. Silence, then, is not harmless - it is surrender.

Every believer carries a story, and every story is a weapon. Your story is your sword. The enemy may try to shame you into silence, but the very scars he meant to destroy you are now your authority to strike him down. Your scars are not a liability; they are your authority.

Testimony as Spiritual Food

Testimony is not just a weapon; it is nourishment. New believers cannot survive on doctrine alone - they need living proof of transformation. Testimony is spiritual food for newborn believers.

David said, *"Come and hear, all ye that fear God, and I will declare what he hath done for my soul"* (Psalm 66:16). To declare is to feed. Teaching may explain, but testimony sustains. Milk makes an audience; meat makes an army - but testimony keeps them alive in between.

Testimony is like manna in the wilderness. Without it, the people faint. With it, they march forward. Churches that silence testimony starve their children. Advertising may catch them, but you won't keep them. Testimony transforms them.

Teaching informs the mind, but testimony ignites the heart. It gives courage to those too weak to fight and hope to those drowning in despair. Testimony is what turns survival into growth.

Transparency and Authority

There is a line that must be shouted: If you can't give your transparent testimony, you are fired. Authority in the Kingdom is inseparable from transparency. Leaders who hide their stories lose their authority. Without testimony, leaders lose their prophetic authority.

Paul did not conceal his struggles. He declared, *"Most gladly therefore will I rather glory in my infirmities, that the power of Christ may rest upon me"* (2 Corinthians 12:9). His testimony was not weakness - it was weaponry. His scars authenticated his authority.

People don't need perfect leaders; they need transparent ones. Hidden pulpits raise hidden people. Silent leaders breed silent congregations. When leaders testify, they release their people to testify.

A leader without testimony is like a shepherd without a voice - the sheep scatter. A hidden testimony is a stolen weapon. And when the shepherd loses his weapon, the flock becomes prey.

Transparency births trust. Testimony births boldness. Together they establish prophetic authority.

The Blood and the Word Together

The blood of the Lamb is perfect, but it demands proclamation. The testimony is powerful, but only because it points back to the blood. Alone, each is incomplete. Together, they destroy the accuser.

Israel's deliverance from Egypt shows this clearly. The blood of the lamb marked their doors and preserved them from death (Exodus 12:13). But their testimony carried that victory into generations: *"When your children ask you, 'What mean ye by this service?' you shall say, 'It is the sacrifice of the Lord's passover'"* (Exodus 12:26–27).

The blood secured them. The testimony sustained them. The blood delivered them. The testimony discipled their children.

The blood is silent until the testimony speaks. The testimony is powerless unless it exalts the blood. Together they break the chains of hell.

Testimony Multiplies Faith

Every testimony is a seed. When planted, it multiplies faith in those who hear it. Your testimony is someone else's prophecy.

When you declare, "God healed me," it prophesies healing to others. When you declare, "God delivered me," it proclaims freedom to those still bound. When you declare, "God restored my family," it births hope for reconciliation in broken homes.

Psalm 119:111 declares, *"Thy testimonies have I taken as an heritage for ever: for they are the rejoicing of my heart."* Testimonies are inheritance - they belong to the people of God as a treasury of encouragement.

Silence is surrender. Boldness is multiplication. The church that silences testimonies cripples its own faith. But the church that celebrates them multiplies courage in every heart.

Like loaves and fishes, testimony multiplies as it is shared. One man's story feeds thousands with faith.

The Enemy Hates Testimony

Satan cannot stand against the power of testimony. He can twist Scripture, but he cannot erase your story. He can argue doctrine, but he cannot refute a life transformed.

This is why shame is his weapon of choice. Shame convinces believers that their past disqualifies them from speaking. But the truth is the opposite: the very thing the devil tries to use to silence you is the very thing God redeems to empower you.

Silence is surrender. Testimony is warfare. When the redeemed declare what God has done, the enemy is exposed and disarmed.

The Psalmist declared, *"Let the redeemed of the Lord say so, whom he hath redeemed from the hand of the enemy"* (Psalm 107:2). To remain silent is to rob God of glory and give the devil space. To speak is to break chains, not just for you, but for others.

Your silence feeds the enemy. Your testimony starves him.

Generational Transfer Through Testimony

Testimony is not only about now - it is the bridge between generations. Legacy is carried through stories. Without testimony, the next generation becomes orphans.

Psalm 78:4 declares, *"We will not hide them from their children, shewing to the generation to come the praises of the Lord, and his strength, and his wonderful works that he hath done."* Testimony ensures inheritance is not lost.

If the next generation never hears your story, they'll never know their inheritance. Sons and daughters do not thrive on sermons alone; they thrive on stories that prove God is real.

You can't disciple from a stage, only from a table - and testimony is what's served at the table. When fathers and mothers share their stories, sons and daughters inherit courage.

Without testimony, legacy dies. With testimony, faith multiplies across generations.

Conclusion: Testimony as Warfare

Testimony is not optional - it is essential. It is food for the young, authority for the leader, a weapon against the enemy, and a legacy for the future.

Revelation 12:11 is not a suggestion - it is a divine strategy. The saints overcame by blood and testimony. Remove either, and victory is lost. But together, they are unstoppable.

Your story is your sword. The blood gives you victory, but your testimony enforces it. Silence is surrender. Boldness is warfare.

The Spirit is calling the church to open its mouth again. To declare. To roar. To feed the children, to confront the enemy, to pass inheritance, to multiply faith. The redeemed must say so.

The trumpet is sounding. The accuser must hear again what the blood has done and what the saints declare. This is how we overcome: by the blood of the Lamb and the word of our testimony.

Scripture Index

Chapter Nine

The Voice of the King – Hearing and Obeying Christ's Command

Introduction

The Kingdom of God does not rest on programs, marketing, or strategies - it rests on the voice of the King. His voice is not optional; it is the foundation. His commands are not suggestions; they are the law of the Kingdom. *"God, who at sundry times and in divers manners spake in time past unto the fathers by the prophets, hath in these last days spoken unto us by his Son"* (Hebrews 1:1–2).

The church is not built on programs; it is built on the King's command. When He speaks, His word is final. To ignore it is not weakness; it is rebellion. To delay it is not caution; it is disobedience. When the King speaks, silence is rebellion.

His sheep are not defined by talent, knowledge, or even zeal - they are defined by whether they recognize His voice. *"My sheep hear my voice, and I know them, and they follow me"* (John 10:27).

The Authority of the King's Voice

From the beginning, creation responded to the voice of the King. *"And God said, Let there be light: and there was light"* (Genesis 1:3). Creation did not negotiate. The stars did not ask for clarification. The seas did not debate. Creation did not negotiate with His voice; it obeyed instantly.

The psalmist declared, *"The voice of the Lord is powerful; the voice of the Lord is full of majesty"* (Psalm 29:4). His voice breaks cedars, shakes the wilderness, and strips forests bare.

His voice is not an opinion - it is law in the Kingdom. When He speaks, excuses die. When He speaks, demons tremble. When He speaks, death itself surrenders.

This is why His voice defines the church. We are not sustained by clever sermons but by divine utterance. If you can't obey the King's voice, you cannot carry the King's authority.

Hearing vs. Listening

There is a difference between hearing noise and recognizing a voice. Many in churches hear sermons, but only sons discern the Shepherd. Jesus said, *"My sheep hear my voice, and I know them, and they follow me"* (John 10:27).

Many sit in church and hear sound, but only sons discern His voice. Sheep know the tone, the heart, and the authority of their shepherd. They don't follow just words; the sheep don't just follow words - they follow the heart behind the voice.

Crowds hear sound. Sons hear direction. Crowds clap for sermons. Disciples obey instructions. One whisper from the King is worth more than a thousand lectures from men.

Recognition requires intimacy. To hear His voice, you must know Him. To follow His commands, you must walk with Him. Without intimacy, you risk mistaking noise for guidance.

The Danger of Strange Voices

Jesus warned, *"A stranger will they not follow, but will flee from him: for they know not the voice of strangers"* (John 10:5).

Strange voices are everywhere. Cultural voices normalize sin. Political voices offer false hope. Religious voices bury life in ritual. Prophetic pretenders mimic His sound without carrying His Spirit.

Every strange voice seeks to scatter, but the King's voice gathers. Sheep that follow strange voices wander into wolves' mouths. Churches that echo strange voices lose their covering.

The voice you obey is the authority you submit to. If you obey fear, fear rules you. If you obey culture, culture shapes you. If you obey the King, the Kingdom governs you.

Hell doesn't need your rebellion; it only needs you to listen to the wrong voice. Disobedience often begins not with denial, but with distraction. This is why discernment is life or death.

Obedience to the Voice

Hearing without obedience is rebellion. James warned, *"But be ye doers of the word, and not hearers only, deceiving your own selves"* (James 1:22).

If you can't obey the King's voice, you can't carry the King's authority. His commands are not optional guidelines. They are the decrees of a King.

Disobedience is not weakness - it is treason. It is declaring that your will is greater than His. To hesitate is to dethrone Him in your heart. Obedience is immediate or it isn't obedience at all. Yet even here, obedience is empowered by the Spirit, not by human striving. The same voice that instructs also enables. (Philippians 2:13)

Jesus said, *"If ye love me, keep my commandments"* (John 14:15). Love is not proven in words, but in obedience. Every revival in history was birthed by radical obedience. Noah obeyed and built an ark. Abraham obeyed and left his homeland. Moses obeyed and confronted Pharaoh. The apostles obeyed and turned the world upside down.

Obedience is the currency of Kingdom authority. Without it, your prayers are empty and your preaching powerless.

The Voice in the Church Today

The tragedy of our age is that many churches no longer echo the King's voice. Entertainment has drowned out prophecy. Opinion has silenced command. Programs fill sanctuaries, but His decrees no longer shake altars.

When pulpits lose the King's voice, the people lose their way. Without His word, sermons are noise. Without His authority, worship is performance.

Silence in the church is disobedience to the King. We are not called to produce noise; we are called to echo heaven. Programs can fill seats, but only His voice can fill hearts.

When testimonies are declared, His voice resounds in transformed lives. When prophecy is spoken, His voice shakes hearts. When Scripture is read with fire, His voice pierces darkness.

One whisper from the King carries more weight than ten thousand sermons from men. The church must tune its ear again to the Shepherd's call, for only His voice can lead us through the chaos of this hour.

Conclusion: The Call to Echo His Voice

The church is not called to echo culture - it is called to echo the King. We are not microphones for society; we are amplifiers for His decrees.

The sheep live because they hear His voice. The church stands because it obeys His command. The Kingdom advances because His people declare His words.

To ignore His voice is to forfeit His presence. To delay His voice is to deny His power. The voice of the King is the heartbeat of the Kingdom.

The Spirit is calling for the church to return to His voice. To silence every strange sound. To tune our ears once again. For when His people hear and obey, nothing can stop the advance of His Kingdom.

Scripture Index

- Hebrews 1:1–2
- John 10:27
- Genesis 1:3
- Psalm 29:4
- Philippians 2:13
- John 10:5
- James 1:22
- John 14:15

Chapter Ten

Obedience Is Not Optional - The Cost of Following the King

Introduction

The Kingdom of God is not a democracy. It is not built on preferences, votes, or debates. It is ruled by a King whose words are commands, not suggestions. The Kingdom is not built on options; it is built on orders.

When the King speaks, delay is disobedience, and disobedience is rebellion. Still, the believer's obedience flows from love, not fear. We obey because we are already sons, not slaves (Galatians 4:6-7). The church does not move forward by opinions but by obedience. Jesus never invited people to admire Him from a distance - He called them to obey His voice and follow Him fully.

Obedience is not optional; it is the oxygen of the Kingdom. Without it, life dies, authority crumbles, and destiny is forfeited.

The Call of Jesus

Jesus never begged for followers - He commanded disciples. When He called Peter and Andrew, He said, *"Follow me, and I will make you fishers of men"* (Matthew 4:19). Immediately, they left their nets. No contracts. No debate. No hesitation.

The first call of the King is not to ministry but to obedience. Discipleship begins not with what you do but with how quickly you obey. Following Christ costs you everything, but disobedience costs even more.

"If any man will come after me, let him deny himself, and take up his cross daily, and follow me" (Luke 9:23). The cross was not jewelry - it was a death sentence. Jesus made it clear: discipleship is not about convenience but crucifixion.

Obedience Is Immediate or It Isn't Obedience

Obedience is not obedience if it is delayed. Delayed obedience is disguised rebellion. Hesitation is the language of rebellion.

Abraham was commanded to sacrifice Isaac, and Scripture says, *"Abraham rose up early in the morning"* (Genesis 22:3). He did not wait. He did not argue. He obeyed immediately, and his obedience opened the door to blessing.

Saul, on the other hand, spared what God told him to destroy. Samuel declared, *"To obey is better than sacrifice, and to hearken than the fat of rams. For rebellion is as the sin of witchcraft, and stubbornness is as iniquity and idolatry"* (1 Samuel 15:22–23).

Partial obedience is total rebellion. God does not bless half-measures; He blesses full surrender. Sacrifice without obedience is witchcraft. Worship without obedience is deception. Service without obedience is idolatry.

The Cost of Discipleship

Jesus never softened the price tag of obedience. *"If any man come to me, and hate not his father, and mother, and wife, and children, and brethren, and sisters, yea, and his own life also, he cannot be my disciple"* (Luke 14:26).

If it costs you nothing, it is not obedience - it is convenience. True discipleship always empties your hands before it fills them again. The cross is not jewelry - it is a death sentence.

Discipleship will cost you relationships, comfort, reputation, and your very life. *"Whosoever doth not bear his cross, and come after me, cannot be my disciple"* (Luke 14:27).

Jesus demanded that His followers count the cost: *"For which of you, intending to build a tower, sitteth not down first, and counteth the cost?"* (Luke 14:28). To obey the King requires absolute surrender.

Why Obedience Releases Authority

Authority flows in the same direction as obedience. The centurion told Jesus, *"I am a man under authority, having soldiers under me: and I say to this man, Go, and he goeth"* (Matthew 8:9). Because he was submitted, he carried authority.

If you are not under the King's voice, you cannot carry the King's power. Authority is not given to the talented but to the obedient. Obedience is the doorway to authority.

Sacrifice without obedience is witchcraft, and leadership without obedience is fraud. Samuel's words still thunder: *"To obey is better than sacrifice"* (1 Samuel 15:22).

An obedient believer is more dangerous to hell than a thousand disobedient preachers. One act of obedience carries more weight in heaven than a thousand empty sermons.

The Danger of Disobedience

Every fall in Scripture is tied to disobedience. Adam and Eve fell not because they lacked provision but because they ignored the command. Israel wandered for forty years not because God lacked power but because they lacked obedience. Saul lost his throne not for lack of zeal but for lack of submission.

Rebellion doesn't begin with shouting - it begins with subtle compromise. Disobedience is choosing your opinion over His command.

Moses declared, *"See, I have set before thee this day life and good, and death and evil; in that I command thee this day to love the Lord thy God, to walk in his ways, and to keep his commandments"* (Deuteronomy 30:15–16). Obedience produces life; disobedience produces death.

Disobedience dethrones kings, destroys destinies, and delays promises. It is not a minor flaw - it is treason against the throne of God.

Obedience and Revival

Revival has never been birthed by talent - it has always been birthed by obedience. One act of obedience can shake nations.

Noah obeyed and built an ark, though rain had never fallen. Abraham obeyed and left his homeland, though he knew not where he was going. Moses obeyed and confronted Pharaoh, though Pharaoh was the most powerful man alive. The apostles obeyed the command to preach, though it cost them everything.

Obedience turns fishermen into apostles and failures into fathers of faith. Revival flows not from the gifted but from the obedient. The Spirit does not anoint rebellion - He anoints surrender.

Conclusion: The King's Command Is Life

The Kingdom is not sustained by preference but by obedience. Jesus is not looking for admirers; He is raising followers. He is not recruiting fans; He is commissioning soldiers.

Obedience is not optional - it is the oxygen of the Kingdom. Obedience is immediate or it isn't obedience at all.

Partial obedience is total rebellion. Sacrifice without obedience is witchcraft. The Kingdom does not negotiate; it commands.

Disciples are not proven by what they know but by what they obey. The voice of the King does not wait for your agreement - it demands your obedience. To ignore His command is to forfeit His presence. To resist His order is to reject His authority.

The King is speaking. The trumpet is sounding. The only question left is this: will we obey?

Scripture Index

Chapter Eleven

The Remnant Rises – A People Set Apart for the King

Introduction

In every generation, when compromise spreads like disease and multitudes bow to the idols of culture, God preserves a remnant. This remnant is small in number but massive in impact. They are heaven's resistance force on earth.

Paul declared, *"Even so then at this present time also there is a remnant according to the election of grace"* (Romans 11:5). Elijah cried out in despair, thinking he was the last faithful one, but the Lord reminded him: "Yet I have left me seven thousand in Israel, all the knees which have not bowed unto Baal" (1 Kings 19:18).

When the crowd bows, the remnant still stands. The remnant is heaven's answer to earth's rebellion. They are not defined by popularity but by purity, not by applause but by allegiance.

The Identity of the Remnant

Who is the remnant? They are the faithful few who refuse to bow. They are not defined by their visibility but by their loyalty.

Isaiah prophesied, *"The remnant shall return, even the remnant of Jacob, unto the mighty God"* (Isaiah 10:21). The remnant is identified not by size but by returning. While others wander, the remnant comes back to covenant.

Remnant people are not defined by popularity but by purity. They are not chosen because they are many but because they are faithful. God measures strength by faithfulness, not numbers.

One remnant believer is more dangerous to hell than ten thousand compromisers. They are the yeast in the dough, the spark in the forest, the seed that carries the future.

The remnant is not fragile - it is fierce. It has survived storms, betrayals, and persecutions. Remnant people are survivors of storms and carriers of covenant.

The Refining of the Remnant

The remnant is always forged in fire. It is tested, purified, and proven. The fire does not destroy the remnant; it defines them.

Malachi declared, *"He shall sit as a refiner and purifier of silver: and he shall purify the sons of Levi"* (Malachi 3:3). Refining is not punishment; it is preparation.

The furnace does not consume the remnant - it consumes their chains. The flames are not their end but their unveiling.

Like Shadrach, Meshach, and Abednego, the remnant declares: *"Be it known unto thee, O king, that we will not serve thy gods"* (Daniel 3:18). They entered the furnace, but instead of destruction, they found the presence of the Fourth Man.

The remnant is fireproof because their loyalty has already been tested. The fire reveals them. It purifies their motives, strengthens their faith, and proves their devotion.

The Separation of the Remnant

The remnant is not called to blend in - it is called to stand apart. They are separated, consecrated, and marked by holiness.

Paul commanded, *"Come out from among them, and be ye separate, saith the Lord, and touch not the unclean thing"* (2 Corinthians 6:17). The remnant understands that compromise kills authority.

A remnant cannot blend with Babylon and still carry Zion's fire. Holiness is the badge of the remnant. They refuse to drink from Babylon's cup or eat from Babylon's table.

Daniel refused the king's food, and heaven honored him. The remnant draws lines that the world mocks but God blesses.

A remnant is not popular - it is set apart. Popularity seeks applause, but the remnant seeks holiness. The crowd blends in to survive; the remnant stands out to confront.

The Assignment of the Remnant

The remnant is not preserved to hide - it is preserved to build. It is heaven's construction crew in the midst of cultural collapse.

Ezra and Nehemiah were part of the remnant that returned from exile. They rebuilt the altar, restored the walls, and reestablished covenant. While the majority had grown comfortable in Babylon, the remnant carried the burden of rebuilding Zion.

When the majority abandons truth, the remnant rebuilds the altar. When worship has been silenced, the remnant raises their voice. When truth has been buried, the remnant digs it out.

The remnant carries the blueprint of heaven when others have forgotten it. They rebuild what has been torn down, not with human strategies but with divine strength.

The assignment of the remnant is not survival but restoration. They carry the presence of God back into the places where compromise once ruled.

The Authority of the Remnant

The authority of the remnant is not in its size but in its alignment with heaven. Gideon's army of thirty-two thousand was reduced to three hundred. With nothing but jars, torches, and obedience, they shattered Midian's power (Judges 7).

Crowds impress the world, but remnants terrify hell.

The authority of the remnant comes not from numbers but from nearness. They walk close to the King, and His authority flows through them.

When God is with the remnant, the enemy's multitude is meaningless. Pharaoh had armies; Moses had obedience. Goliath had size; David had covenant. Jezebel had prophets; Elijah had fire.

One remnant church can shift the atmosphere of a city. One remnant cry can change the destiny of a nation.

Authority flows to the remnant because they have no agenda but His. Obedience is the language of authority, and the remnant speaks it fluently.

The Rise of the Remnant in Our Generation

We live in a generation drowning in compromise, corruption, and confusion. Yet even now, God is raising a remnant.

The remnant of this generation is marked by holiness - they refuse to bow to the idols of greed, lust, and pride. They are marked by courage - they will not retreat in the face of persecution. They are marked by obedience - they will not debate the King's command; they will obey it.

The remnant is not hidden in fear; it rises in fire.

This generation does not need another crowd - it needs a remnant. A people who will carry the torch of truth, the fire of holiness, and the power of obedience.

The remnant is not intimidated by culture; it confronts it with conviction. They do not hide in survival mode - they rise in revival fire.

The Spirit is summoning the remnant in our day. The question is not whether God will raise one; the question is whether you will be part of it.

Conclusion: A People Set Apart

The remnant rises - not hidden, not silenced, not compromised. They rise purified by fire, separated by holiness, assigned to rebuild, and armed with authority.

The fire does not destroy the remnant; it defines them.

God doesn't need a crowd to win a battle; He needs a remnant.

A remnant is not popular - it is set apart.

When the majority bows, the remnant builds.

The remnant does not survive culture; it confronts culture.

The remnant is small in number but massive in impact.

The future of nations is often hidden in the faithfulness of a remnant.

Hell trembles not at the multitude but at the remnant set apart for the King.

This is the identity, the refining, the separation, the assignment, the authority, and the rising of the remnant. God has always preserved one. The question is: will you be counted among them?

Scripture Index

- Romans 11:5
- 1 Kings 19:18
- Isaiah 10:21
- Malachi 3:3
- Daniel 3:18
- 2 Corinthians 6:17
- Ezra 1:5–6;
- Nehemiah 2:17
- Judges 7

Chapter Twelve

Repentance – The Forgotten Door

Introduction

The Kingdom of God begins with repentance. It is not the end of the journey but the very first step. Without repentance, there is no entry, no growth, and no revival.

"From that time Jesus began to preach, and to say, Repent: for the kingdom of heaven is at hand" (Matthew 4:17). Before miracles, before parables, before the Sermon on the Mount - Jesus thundered one word: Repent.

Repentance is not old-fashioned; it is eternal. It is not the optional add-on to the gospel; it is the very heart of the gospel. The first word of the Kingdom is not love - it is repent. Without repentance, even love cannot be received, for the heart is still hardened in rebellion.

Repentance is the forgotten door, but it is the only door.

Repentance: Heaven's First Command

Repentance is heaven's first command to mankind. John the Baptist came preaching, *"Repent ye: for the kingdom of heaven is at hand"* (Matthew 3:2). Jesus Himself began His ministry with the same demand. Peter stood at Pentecost and declared, *"Repent, and be baptized every one of you in the name of Jesus Christ for the remission of sins"* (Acts 2:38).

Every prophet, every revival, every awakening began with one word: repent. The first call of heaven is not comfort - it is correction.

Repentance is not an altar call - it is a lifestyle. It is the ongoing doorway of discipleship. You do not graduate from repentance - you grow by it.

You cannot bypass the door of repentance and expect Kingdom life. You cannot sidestep it and expect Kingdom authority. The gospel without repentance is powerless, for it never changes the heart.

The Forgotten Door

Repentance is the forgotten door in much of today's church. It has been replaced by self-help, affirmation, and motivational speeches. Yet without repentance, there is no salvation, no transformation, no revival.

Jesus warned the church in Revelation: *"Remember therefore from whence thou art fallen, and repent, and do the first works"* (Revelation 2:5). Even churches themselves can lose their lampstand when they abandon repentance.

The modern church has traded repentance for relevance, and in doing so, lost its authority. You cannot preach Kingdom without demanding repentance.

122

Repentance does not excuse sin - it executes it. It kills rebellion at the root and dethrones pride from the heart. Anything less is cosmetic change, religion painted over rebellion.

The world says, "Don't change - just be you." The King says, "Repent - for only then can you become Mine."

What True Repentance Looks Like

True repentance is not sorrow alone. Paul declared, *"Godly sorrow worketh repentance to salvation not to be repented of: but the sorrow of the world worketh death"* (2 Corinthians 7:10).

Worldly sorrow cries, but never changes. Godly sorrow produces transformation. Repentance does not feel bad and stay the same - it turns and never looks back.

Repentance is not crying at an altar - it is changing at an altar. It is not just emotion but decision. Repentance does not reform sin - it removes it. Repentance does not negotiate with rebellion - it crucifies it.

John the Baptist thundered, *"Bring forth fruits meet for repentance"* (Matthew 3:8). Real repentance produces fruit: holiness, integrity, and visible change.

Repentance is the execution of sin, the burial of the old man, the resurrection of new life.

The Cost of Neglecting Repentance

When repentance is neglected, sin festers, the heart hardens, and judgment follows.

Israel refused to repent, and the prophets wept over their rebellion. Jeremiah declared, *"This is a nation that obeyeth not the voice of the Lord their God, nor receiveth correction: truth is perished, and is cut off from their mouth"* (Jeremiah 7:28).

When repentance is silenced, rebellion multiplies. Excuses are the enemy of repentance. Saul lost his kingdom not because he sinned, but because he excused his sin. He said, "The people made me do it." Excuses are rebellion dressed in religious language.

The refusal to repent is the fastest way to judgment. Repentance is the mercy of God extended before the hammer falls. To neglect it is to invite destruction.

Repentance and Revival

Every revival in history has been birthed by repentance. Nineveh repented at Jonah's preaching, and God spared the city. *"And God saw their works, that they turned from their evil way; and God repented of the evil"* (Jonah 3:10).

John the Baptist prepared the way for Christ by preaching repentance. The Spirit was poured out at Pentecost after Peter's command to repent.

No repentance, no revival. Say it again until it burns into your soul: no repentance, no revival.

Revival begins not at the stage of performance but at the altar of repentance. It does not begin with talent but with tears. Repentance breaks the ground for the rain of the Spirit.

Every move of God has a sound, and it is the sound of weeping at the altar, the sound of a people turning back to God.

Repentance as a Lifestyle

Repentance is not a one-time event; it is the rhythm of the Kingdom. Luther was right when he wrote: "The whole of a Christian's life is repentance." (Luther, 1962)

Repentance is not weakness - it is warfare. It disarms pride, dethrones idols, and destroys sin. Repentance is not shame - it is freedom. It does not chain you to your past; it cuts the chains and frees you for your future.

David prayed, *"Create in me a clean heart, O God; and renew a right spirit within me"* (Psalm 51:10). His prayer was not a moment but a lifestyle.

Repentance is not a pit stop; it is the highway of holiness. Those who walk it live in continual renewal, continual cleansing, continual alignment.

Repentance keeps the conscience sharp and the heart tender. It positions the believer for constant victory.

Conclusion: Reopening the Forgotten Door

Repentance is the forgotten door, but it is the only door. Without it, there is no entry into the Kingdom. Without it, there is no revival in the church. Without it, there is no transformation in the believer.

Repentance is not optional - it is oxygen.

Repentance is not an altar call - it is a lifestyle.

You cannot bypass the door of repentance and expect Kingdom life.

Repentance does not excuse sin - it executes it.

No repentance, no revival.

Repentance is not a pit stop; it is the highway of holiness.

If the church will repent, the world will awaken.

The Spirit is calling the church back to the place of tears, back to the altar of surrender, back to the forgotten door. The King is speaking. The door is open. The only question is: will we walk through?

Scripture Index

Chapter Thirteen

Truth That Divides – The Sword of the King's Word

Introduction

The Kingdom of God is not built on slogans or suggestions - it is built on unshakable truth. Jesus did not simply speak truth; He is Truth. *"I am the way, the truth, and the life"* (John 14:6). To encounter Him is to collide with reality itself.

The gospel does not blur lines; it draws them. It does not soothe rebellion; it slices it open. Truth is not a pillow - it is a plow, cutting deep into the hardened ground of human pride and exposing the roots of deception.

From the beginning, truth has divided. Noah preached righteousness while a world of millions drowned in their rebellion. Elijah stood against the prophets of Baal, declaring, *"How long halt ye between two opinions? if the Lord be God, follow him: but if Baal, then follow him"* (1 Kings 18:21). Truth drew the line, and fire from heaven confirmed it.

Jesus warned, *"Think not that I am come to send peace on earth: I came not to send peace, but a sword"* (Matthew 10:34). Truth does not whisper - it roars. It forces decision. It demands allegiance.

Truth that does not cut is not truth at all.

The Sword of Truth

The Word of God is not a decorative prop - it is a lethal weapon. *"For the word of God is quick, and powerful, and sharper than any two-edged sword"* (Hebrews 4:12). Like the Roman soldier's gladius, short and double-edged, it was crafted not for show but for precision in close combat.

When the Word is wielded, hell is wounded. Demons scatter, chains shatter, captives are released. The Word is not for display in pulpits - it is for battle in the trenches of life. A preacher without a sword is a soldier without a weapon.

Isaiah thundered, *"So shall my word be that goeth forth out of my mouth: it shall not return unto me void"* (Isaiah 55:11). His Word always accomplishes. It never fails.

John saw Jesus in Revelation: *"Out of his mouth went a sharp twoedged sword"* (Revelation 1:16). The Word is His weapon, and when we declare it, we wield the same sword. The Word in your mouth is the same sword that was in His.

Compromise dulls the sword; obedience keeps it sharp. A dull church produces dull disciples, but a sharp church terrifies hell.

Truth Is Not Neutral

Truth is never passive - it is aggressive against lies. *"Ye shall know the truth, and the truth shall make you free"* (John 8:32). Freedom never comes without confrontation.

Truth takes sides - it never stays silent. To refuse to speak truth is to agree with lies. Neutrality in a war of truth is betrayal. Neutral ground is devil's ground.

Pilate tried neutrality when he said, "I find no fault in him," yet handed Jesus over. That neutrality condemned him. Israel wavered at Mount Carmel until Elijah forced them to choose. Joshua declared, "Choose you this day whom ye will serve" (Joshua 24:15). Truth always demands decision.

Paul warned, *"The time will come when they will not endure sound doctrine"* (2 Timothy 4:3). That time is now. Culture craves affirmation, not transformation. But affirmation without repentance is bondage in disguise.

Silence in the face of deception is treason against truth.

Division by Design

Jesus said plainly, *"I am come to set a man at variance against his father, and the daughter against her mother… and a man's foes shall be they of his own household"* (Matthew 10:35–36). The sword of truth divides by design.

This is not chaos - it is clarity. The sword does not bring confusion; it brings clarity. Jesus does not divide to destroy; He divides to reveal allegiance.

When Moses cried, *"Who is on the Lord's side?"* (Exodus 32:26), truth demanded separation. Some stepped forward; others stood exposed as rebels. Amos asked, *"Can two walk together, except*

129

they be agreed?" (Amos 3:3). Division is not destruction - it is preservation.

Truth is the great separator of sheep from goats, light from darkness, remnant from rebel. When Jesus draws the line, you cannot straddle it.

Truth Against Culture

Culture applauds compromise; the Kingdom demands conviction. Isaiah warned, *"Woe unto them that call evil good, and good evil"* (Isaiah 5:20).

Culture shifts like sand, but truth stands like stone. Joseph refused to bow to Egypt's corruption. Daniel would not defile himself with Babylon's table. The apostles declared, *"We ought to obey God rather than men"* (Acts 5:29).

Truth is not a trend - it is eternal. The world edits morality, but the Word establishes it forever. Jesus prayed, *"Sanctify them through thy truth: thy word is truth"* (John 17:17). Truth sanctifies, purifies, and separates.

When culture rewrites morality, the remnant rewrites culture with truth. Truth is not a trend; it is a throne. The church is not called to echo culture - it is called to confront it with a sword.

These scriptures point to a truth:

- Colossians 2:8 *Beware lest any man spoil you through philosophy and vain deceit, after the tradition of men, after the rudiments of the world, and not after Christ.*

- Numbers 23:19 *God is not a man, that he should lie; neither the son of man, that he should repent: hath he said, and shall he not do it? or hath he spoken, and shall he not make it good?*

- Malachi 3:6 *For I am the LORD, I change not; therefore ye sons of Jacob are not consumed.*

- Hebrews 13:8 *Jesus Christ the same yesterday, and to day, and for ever.*

Prophetic insight: God does not change and does not change to meet your cultural rules. You changed to have a relationship with him and abandoned the cultural rules of the world that enslaved you.

The Offense of Truth

Truth offends, and it is meant to. Peter declared that Christ is *"a stone of stumbling, and a rock of offence"* (1 Peter 2:8).

If truth never offends, it is not truth - it is flattery. If truth doesn't pierce you, it cannot purify you.

The cross is offensive because it demands death before resurrection. Truth confronts comfort before it brings freedom.

Jesus looked at the rich young ruler and demanded surrender, and he walked away sorrowful. John the Baptist rebuked Herod for adultery, and it cost him his head. Paul asked, *"Am I therefore become your enemy, because I tell you the truth?"* (Galatians 4:16).

Truth does not negotiate; it demands. It demands repentance, surrender, and obedience. The Pharisees killed Jesus because His truth exposed their hypocrisy. Pilate mocked truth while Truth Himself stood before him.

The sword of truth is offensive to rebels, but life to the remnant.

Living by the Sword

To live by truth is to live under fire. Jesus said, *"If any man will come after me, let him deny himself, and take up his cross, and follow me"* (Matthew 16:24).

Living by the sword means living misunderstood but never defeated. Truth may exile you from men, but it enthrones you with God.

Paul charged Timothy, *"Preach the word; be instant in season, out of season"* (2 Timothy 4:2). Those who carry the sword must never sheath it when culture resists.

Ephesians 6:17 calls it *"the sword of the Spirit, which is the word of God."* Those who wield it may bleed by it, but they will also build with it. The apostles were beaten, imprisoned, and martyred, but their obedience carved out the church that still stands today.

132

Those who carry the sword will often bleed by it, but they will also conquer with it. Truth may cost you friends, but it gains you freedom.

If you dull the sword, you betray the King. If you wield the sword, you terrify hell.

Conclusion: The Sword That Saves

Truth is not a suggestion - it is a sword. It is not a whisper - it is a weapon. The church does not advance by hiding the sword but by swinging it.

The sword that divides families also delivers nations. The sword that exposes rebellion also establishes righteousness. Revelation warns the churches: *"Repent; or else I will come unto thee quickly, and will fight against them with the sword of my mouth"* (Revelation 2:16).

Truth that does not cut is not truth at all.

Truth is not optional - it is the dividing line of the Kingdom.

Truth may wound first, but it heals forever.

The sword that divides today will deliver tomorrow.

The King's Word is unsheathed. The sword of truth is swinging. The question is not whether it will fall - but where you will stand when it does.

Scripture Index

Chapter Fourteen

When Identity Is Rebuilt

Introduction - Reconstructing the Ruins

God never leaves His people in ruins. He rebuilds. He restores. He renames. He reclaims. *"And they shall build the old wastes, they shall raise up the former desolations, and they shall repair the waste cities, the desolations of many generations"* (Isaiah 61:4).

The enemy's first weapon is always identity theft. From Eden, the serpent's question - "Did God really say?" - was not just about fruit but about identity. If the enemy can rename you, he can reassign you.

Adam and Eve fell because they doubted the identity God had given them: image-bearers of the Most High. Noah stood against a flood generation because he knew his identity as a righteous man before God. Abraham left his homeland because he believed the identity God declared over him: father of many nations. Moses stood before Pharaoh because he embraced his calling not as Egypt's prince but as God's prophet.

Identity is the battleground of destiny. When you forget who God says you are, you will live as a slave to what the world calls you. But when God rebuilds, He does not patch cracks - He lays new foundations. Identity is the foundation of obedience, and obedience is the foundation of destiny.

The Ruin of False Identity

Sin always distorts identity. Babylon never builds - it always brands. Daniel and his friends were renamed Belteshazzar, Shadrach, Meshach, and Abednego. This was not random; it was identity warfare. Babylon sought to erase their covenant names and instill compromise. That is the strategy of every false system: strip away identity to control destiny.

False identity locks you in prisons where the doors are already open. You wear labels that God never placed on you: addict, failure, worthless, forgotten. Every lie you believe about yourself is a chain the enemy didn't even have to fasten.

When Israel forgot they were chosen, they bowed to idols. When the prodigal forgot he was a son, he fed pigs like a slave. When Gideon hid in fear, calling himself the least in his father's house, God declared, *"The Lord is with thee, thou mighty man of valour"* (Judges 6:12). Heaven saw identity even when earth saw weakness.

False identity is the enemy's counterfeit covenant. It offers temporary labels but steals eternal destiny. But the King has not abandoned His covenant. He rebuilds the ruins. He strips off false labels. He restores His decree.

The King's Blueprint for Identity

The King never leaves His children guessing. He speaks identity over them with heaven's authority. *"Ye have not received the spirit of bondage again to fear; but ye have received the Spirit of adoption, whereby we cry, Abba, Father"* (Romans 8:15).

Identity is not discovered - it is received. Identity is not your opinion of yourself - it is the King's decree over you. You don't define yourself; the Father defines you.

At Jesus' baptism, the heavens opened and the Father said, *"This is my beloved Son, in whom I am well pleased"* (Matthew 3:17). Notice: this declaration came before any miracle, before any sermon, before the cross. Heaven calls you son before earth sees your fruit.

Paul wrote, *"The Spirit itself beareth witness with our spirit, that we are the children of God"* (Romans 8:16). The Spirit of adoption doesn't suggest - you belong, period.

Heaven names you while earth still doubts you. Identity is the blueprint of destiny. Without it, purpose collapses. With it, you can stand against Babylon and walk into destiny unshaken.

The Power of Renaming

When God restores identity, He often renames. Abram became Abraham. Jacob became Israel. Simon became Peter. Saul became Paul. Heaven's renaming is not cosmetic - it is covenantal.

When God renames you, He reclaims you. When heaven calls you by a new name, hell loses its claim.

Abram lived childless, but God declared, *"Thy name shall be Abraham; for a father of many nations have I made thee"* (Genesis 17:5). The name was bigger than his barrenness.

Jacob wrestled all night with God, and the angel declared, *"Thy name shall be called no more Jacob, but Israel: for as a prince hast thou power with God and with men"* (Genesis 32:28). No longer deceiver - now covenant carrier.

Jesus looked at Simon, unstable and impulsive, and declared, *"Thou art Peter, and upon this rock I will build my church"* (Matthew 16:18). Heaven named him for his future, not his failures.

Revelation 2:17 promises, *"To him that overcometh will I give... a white stone, and in the stone a new name written."* Renaming is the King's declaration that the old you no longer exists. The remnant carries names written in heaven, not labels stamped by Babylon.

Identity Rebuilt Through the Word

James wrote, *"For if any be a hearer of the word, and not a doer, he is like unto a man beholding his natural face in a glass"* (James 1:23). The Word of God is the mirror of true identity.

Babylon's mirror reflects shame. The world's mirror reflects failure. But the Word is the mirror that shows you not who you were, but who you are becoming.

138

The Word does not show you your reflection - it shows you your resurrection. Every decree dismantles a lie of Babylon. Every page reveals a name heaven calls you. The mirror of the Word uncovers the masterpiece beneath the rubble.

Jeremiah 1:5 declares, *"Before I formed thee in the belly I knew thee; and before thou camest forth out of the womb I sanctified thee."* God's Word reveals identity written before time began.

Every time you open the Word, heaven whispers your name again. You cannot carry Kingdom authority with Babylon's identity still on you. The Word strips labels of failure and clothes you in robes of righteousness. The mirror of the Word reveals the masterpiece beneath the rubble.

Identity Rebuilt in Community

Identity is not rebuilt in isolation. Israel returned from exile not as scattered individuals but as a remnant. Ezra and Nehemiah led them in rebuilding together - altars restored, walls rebuilt, covenant renewed.

Ezra 3:10–11 records, *"When the builders laid the foundation of the temple of the Lord, they set the priests in their apparel with trumpets... and they sang together by course in praising and giving thanks unto the Lord."* Their identity was rebuilt as their foundation was laid.

You don't rebuild alone - you rebuild with the remnant. Identity is rebuilt in the presence of the King and in the company of His people.

Isolation distorts identity; community restores it. Every wall Nehemiah rebuilt shouted: "We are still His people!"

The early church knew this. *"They continued steadfastly in the apostles' doctrine and fellowship, and in breaking of bread, and in prayers"* (Acts 2:42). Their identity was forged in covenant community. Identity isolated is fragile; identity in community is unbreakable.

Living in Rebuilt Identity

When identity is rebuilt, authority is restored. The prodigal son came home filthy and broken, but the father clothed him in a robe, placed a ring on his hand, and sandals on his feet (Luke 15:22). The robe covered shame. The ring restored authority. The sandals marked him as a son, not a slave.

Authority flows where identity is secure. You cannot roar like a lion while believing you're still a slave.

The robe of righteousness, the ring of covenant, and the sandals of sonship are not ornaments - they are orders to reign. Galatians 4:7 declares, *"Wherefore thou art no more a servant, but a son; and if a son, then an heir of God through Christ."* Sons don't beg for bread - they sit at the table.

The remnant is rising, clothed in rebuilt identity, walking in sonship, carrying the authority of heaven. Their restored identity is not for survival - it is for dominion.

Conclusion: Identity Rebuilt for Destiny

Identity is not recovered - it is rebuilt on Christ alone. God is raising a people who know who they are - not what Babylon called them, but what heaven names them.

When God renames you, He reclaims you.

Identity is not discovered - it is received.

The Word is the mirror that shows you not who you were, but who you are becoming.

You cannot carry Kingdom authority with Babylon's identity still on you.

Identity is rebuilt in the presence of the King and in the company of His people.

The Spirit is renaming a generation so they can reclaim a destiny.

Revelation 3:12 promises: *"Him that overcometh will I make a pillar in the temple of my God... and I will write upon him my new name."*

Rebuilt identity is not for display - it is for dominion. When identity is rebuilt, authority is restored, and the Kingdom advances. The ruins are raised. The sons and daughters stand. The remnant rises - rebuilt, renamed, and ready.

Scripture Index

- Isaiah 61:4
- Genesis 3:1–5
- Genesis 6:9
- Genesis 12:1–3
- Exodus 3:10–12
- Daniel 1:7
- Judges 6:12
- Romans 8:15–16
- Matthew 3:17
- Genesis 17:5
- Genesis 32:28
- Matthew 16:18
- Acts 9:4–15
- Revelation 2:17
- James 1:23–25
- Jeremiah 1:5
- Ezra 3:10–11
- Nehemiah 2:17–18
- Acts 2:42
- Luke 15:22
- Galatians 4:7
- 1 Peter 2:9
- Revelation 3:12

Chapter Fifteen

Walking in Kingdom Authority– Living as Ambassadors of the King

Introduction

Authority is not a suggestion of the Kingdom - it is its very atmosphere. To walk with the King is to walk in His authority. Jesus declared, *"All power is given unto me in heaven and in earth"* (Matthew 28:18). He then turned to His disciples and gave them the commission to go, teach, heal, deliver, and disciple nations.

The Kingdom does not give permission; it gives power. Power to bind, to loose, to heal, to deliver, to proclaim the gospel with boldness. Authority is not optional - it is the mark of true discipleship.

Luke 10:19 confirms this: *"Behold, I give unto you power to tread on serpents and scorpions, and over all the power of the enemy: and nothing shall by any means hurt you."* The King equips His people not to survive but to rule.

Authority is not a luxury of the church; it is its birthright. But birthright only becomes reality when embraced by faith and obedience.

The Source of Kingdom Authority

All true authority flows from the King Himself. *"All power is given unto me,"* Jesus declared (Matthew 28:18). Authority is never self-made. It is received, not earned.

Jesus modeled this in His earthly walk. He declared, *"The Son can do nothing of himself, but what he seeth the Father do"* (John 5:19). His authority flowed from His submission.

Delegated authority is only as strong as your submission. If you resist submission, you resist authority. James 4:7 says, *"Submit yourselves therefore to God. Resist the devil, and he will flee from you."* Resistance flows from submission. Authority flows from alignment.

This is why rebellion always destroys authority. Lucifer lost his place not for lack of power but for lack of submission. Saul lost his kingdom because he valued sacrifice above obedience. Authority that is not rooted in submission becomes witchcraft disguised as leadership.

And authority is never given for manipulation. It is not for testing or trapping men - that belongs to God alone. *"I the Lord search the heart, I try the reins, even to give every man according to his ways"* (Jeremiah 17:10). Authority is not license to create artificial tests for the people of God. It is not to be used as a net to ensnare but as a staff to shepherd.

Authority is also not a tool for gossip or slander. To weaponize words is to forfeit true authority. *"Thou shalt not go up* and down as a talebearer among thy people" (Leviticus 19:16). A warning in the book of Psalms: "*Whoso privily slandereth his neighbour, him will I cut off: him that hath an high look and a proud heart will not I suffer.*" (Psalms 101:5) Paul warns that "*neither fornicators, nor idolaters, nor adulterers… nor thieves, nor covetous, nor drunkards, nor revilers*" will inherit the Kingdom of God (1 Corinthians 6:9–10). The word *revilers* describes those who weaponize their words - people who use their tongues to tear down people and what God is building. To revile is more than to insult; it is to curse what Heaven has blessed and to speak death where God has spoken life. Scripture calls such speech corrupt and warns that it defiles both the speaker and the hearer. Revilers are those who misuse the authority of their voice, turning it from edification to destruction. But the speech of the righteous builds; it heals, restores, and defends the truth. "*Let no corrupt communication proceed out of your mouth, but that which is good to the use of edifying*" (Ephesians 4:29). To collect information secretly, to build files against the sheep, to use words as weapons - this is not oversight, it is predatory, and it is condemned.

In Scripture, **Nehemiah** faced this spirit through **Sanballat and Tobiah,** men who mocked, slandered, and conspired against the rebuilding of Jerusalem's walls. They laughed him to scorn, saying, "*What is this thing that ye do? Will ye rebel against the king?*" (Nehemiah 2:19). Later, their ridicule turned into open threats: "*What do these feeble Jews? Will they fortify themselves?... Even*

145

that which they build, if a fox go up, he shall even break down their stone wall" (Nehemiah 4:2–3).

Yet Nehemiah did not descend into their argument. He discerned that their mockery was not merely human - it was demonic opposition against divine purpose. His response was prayer and persistence: *"Nevertheless we made our prayer unto our God, and set a watch against them day and night"* (Nehemiah 4:9). When revilers shouted, Nehemiah built. When they cursed, he prayed. When they plotted, he strengthened the people's hands for the work.

The lesson is eternal: the spirit of Sanballat still rises wherever something holy is being rebuilt. Revilers appear at the gate of restoration, not to destroy with swords, but with words. They attempt to discourage builders, distort motives, and discredit leadership. But the Kingdom builder must do as Nehemiah did - keep his hands on the wall and his heart before God.

The voice of revilers cannot halt what heaven has decreed. Their words will fall powerless, but the words of the faithful will endure. *"Let no corrupt communication proceed out of your mouth, but that which is good to the use of edifying, that it may minister grace unto the hearers"* (Ephesians 4:29).

This same spirit still operates today, even at the altar of God. It slithers in like the serpent of old - religious, subtle, and cloaked in false discernment. You can see it when a man prays with a woman - or a woman with a man - at a public altar, and a whispering spirit begins to move through the congregation: "We must stop this before it becomes an affair," or "Their motives aren't pure," or "It just doesn't look right." These whispers sound holy, but they are poison. They are not discernment; they are accusation. The very premise carries corruption, for it seeks to smear character and sow suspicion under the disguise of concern.

This is not the Spirit of God - it is the spirit of Sanballat reborn in religious garments. It hides behind Scripture but violates its spirit, twisting the Word into a weapon of division. Jesus Himself exposed this deception when He ministered openly to the woman at the well. While religious minds would have called it "improper," Heaven called it redemption. The same lying spirit that once accused the Son of God now whispers in modern churches to hinder restoration and halt growth.

I have seen this spirit split congregations and suffocate revival. It creeps in quietly, spreading distrust among those God is trying to knit together. But once it is confronted and rebuked, the atmosphere clears, unity returns, and growth begins again.

The antidote is discernment anchored in the fruit of the Spirit - especially patience and self-control. It takes time to track this type of spirit down to the people involved, but with patience, you can find them; they tend to get brazen as you are patient, and they will slip up and reveal themselves. For when this spirit is exposed, you will need restraint and wisdom to deal with those entangled by it. Do not fight flesh; address the spirit. Do not answer accusation with accusation; answer it with truth and authority. For what is built in love must be protected from the whisper of the serpent. (There is more detail about this in chapter sixteen, the dream about the rabbits.)

Even partial disclosure is deception. Half-truths are whole lies when they are designed to manipulate. *"Lying lips are abomination to the Lord: but they that deal truly are his delight"* (Proverbs 12:22). Authority that twists information to control a narrative has already abandoned truth, and when truth is abandoned, authority evaporates. This is the easiest way to catch church leaders up in sin. Because leaders believe they are protecting people with this sin, but in reality, they make the issue worse once it is discovered, and lose people in the congregation, and now an offense is created due to whole lies disguised as partial truth.

Many times you will see this same pattern unfold in ministry. A person, a leader, or even an entire ministry group begins to attack another work of God - not with open confrontation, but with whispers. They will say, "You should stay away from that person or that group; it will make you look bad," or, "You shouldn't be around them - they're mostly men," or, "They're mostly women." One of the most subtle lies is, "You should only fellowship with people in your own age group." That statement sounds harmless, but it is the spirit of ministry envy dressed in religious reasoning.

The truth is, teens should desire to be around adult ministries - that's how they learn, that's how they mature. Isolation among peers breeds immaturity. Keeping teens among teens only is insanity; it delays their growth and robs them of the wisdom of those who have walked further. Yet this tactic works well for those who want to malign another ministry. They make it sound as though the other group is dangerous, tainted, or "off" in some spiritual way. Then they add another poisonous line to make it sound credible: "I can't really talk about it, but I know some things." It's the counterfeit voice of discernment - a voice that tries to pretend it carries inside information from someone in authority, when in truth, it carries nothing but deception.

This is how the serpent speaks in the house of God. It whispers through the mouths of the immature, attempting to divide what God has joined together. These kinds of statements are not birthed from discernment - they are born from jealousy. One ministry begins to fail, to shrink, or to struggle, while another begins to bear fruit. Instead of repenting or learning, envy speaks. It uses gossip as its weapon and pretends that destruction is discernment.

But the Spirit of the Lord says - use discernment, not division. The fruit will always expose the root. If you will stay silent and patient, the Spirit will reveal what words try to hide. People who gossip always talk; those who walk in the Spirit wait and watch. Sometimes the wisest move is to pretend ignorance so the full pattern of deception can unfold before your eyes. A quiet spirit carries authority, and in stillness, the source of the problem is revealed.

And here is the truth every believer must learn early: do not be offended by the sinner in a church. Wherever you go - whether on the street or in the sanctuary - you will find sin. The church is not a museum for the perfect; it is a hospital for the wounded. The first lesson I teach anyone stepping into ministry is this: don't let the presence of sin in others make you abandon the presence of God in yourself. The wheat and the tares grow together until the harvest (Matthew 13:30). The Spirit of discernment does not condemn - it intercedes. It does not gossip - it restores.

Prophetic insight: if you are preaching the true Gospel of the Kingdom, it will always work. It will multiply, transform, and bear fruit. But if you preach the wrong gospel - or preach the right gospel in the wrong spirit - it will not be received, and it will not produce. The problem is not always the soil; sometimes it is the seed. When you see a work failing, do not rush to criticize it; instead, examine what spirit it was sown in. The proof is always in the fruit.

The authority of the Kingdom is not surveillance - it is service. It does not gather secrets to crush the sheep - it lays down its life to protect them. Jesus said, *"I am the good shepherd: the good shepherd giveth his life for the sheep"* (John 10:11).

Authority Restored Through Christ

Adam forfeited authority in Eden when he yielded to the serpent's lie. Humanity's crown was cast into the dust, and dominion was traded for slavery.

But Christ came as the second Adam to restore what was lost. *"Let them have dominion over the fish of the sea, and over the fowl of the air, and over the cattle, and over all the earth"* (Genesis 1:26). That mandate was never revoked - it was restored at Calvary.

Paul wrote, *"For if by one man's offence death reigned by one; much more they which receive abundance of grace and of the gift of righteousness shall reign in life by one, Jesus Christ"* (Romans 5:17).

Calvary was not just about forgiveness - it was about restoration of dominion. The cross was not only the removal of sin but the restoration of authority. When Jesus declared, *"It is finished"* (John 19:30), He was not only ending sin's hold - He was reclaiming heaven's authority for earth's ambassadors.

Walking in Delegated Authority

The church has not been called to observe the Kingdom but to enforce it. Jesus said, *"I will give unto thee the keys of the kingdom of heaven: and whatsoever thou shalt bind on earth shall be bound in heaven: and whatsoever thou shalt loose on earth shall be loosed in heaven"* (Matthew 16:19).

Authority unused is authority lost. Keys are useless if they remain in your pocket. They are given to open, to lock, to protect, to release. The Kingdom has placed keys in the hands of the church.

Jesus called the twelve together and *"gave them power and authority over all devils, and to cure diseases. And he sent them to preach the kingdom of God, and to heal the sick"* (Luke 9:1–2). Authority was not given for titles - it was given for tasks.

In Acts 3:6–8, Peter looked at the lame man at the gate and declared, *"Silver and gold have I none; but such as I have give I thee: In the name of Jesus Christ of Nazareth rise up and walk."* Authority was demonstrated not by wealth but by the Word.

The Cost of Kingdom Authority

Authority cannot be divorced from holiness. You cannot rebuke what you secretly entertain. Authority requires obedience, humility, and submission.

In Acts 19:13–16, the sons of Sceva attempted to cast out demons *"by Jesus whom Paul preacheth."* The spirit answered, *"Jesus I know, and Paul I know; but who are ye?"* The counterfeit was exposed. Authority cannot be borrowed - it must be birthed in obedience.

You cannot rebuke what you secretly entertain. A compromised life produces compromised authority. Holiness is not optional - it is the soil in which authority grows.

Jesus said, *"Behold, the prince of this world cometh, and hath nothing in me"* (John 14:30). His authority flowed from His purity. Authority is expensive - it will cost you comfort, compromise, and carnality.

Kingdom Authority in Spiritual Warfare

Authority is given for warfare, but not against flesh and blood. Paul declared, *"For the weapons of our warfare are not carnal, but mighty through God to the pulling down of strong holds"* (2 Corinthians 10:4).

Spiritual authority is not shouting louder - it is standing stronger. It is not volume that moves demons but alignment. Authority is not intimidation - it is incarnation.

Paul exhorts the church: *"Put on the whole armour of God, that ye may be able to stand against the wiles of the devil"* (Ephesians 6:11). Authority requires armour. Truth girds your loins. Righteousness covers your heart. Faith shields you. The Word becomes your sword.

Authority is exercised not in theory but in confrontation. Authority is proven not in pulpits but in battlefields.

Living as Ambassadors of the King

Paul wrote, *"Now then we are ambassadors for Christ, as though God did beseech you by us"* (2 Corinthians 5:20). An ambassador does not speak his own mind - he speaks for his King.

153

Your authority is not in your opinion but in His commission. *"As my Father hath sent me, even so send I you"* (John 20:21).

Ambassadors live under a different government. They are not subject to the economy, laws, or culture of the nation they live in, but of the kingdom they represent. Authority is tied to representation.

Ambassadors do not negotiate - they represent. Ambassadors do not compromise - they declare. The church must recover its ambassadorial role - not echoing Babylon but representing Zion.

Conclusion: Authority for Assignment

Authority is not for show - it is for assignment. It is not given to inflate egos but to advance the Kingdom.

Authority is not a title; it is a trust. Revelation 4:10 describes elders casting their crowns before the throne. The Kingdom gives no crowns to keep - only crowns to cast.

Acts 1:8 declares, *"Ye shall receive power, after that the Holy Ghost is come upon you: and ye shall be witnesses unto me."* Authority is not given for comfort but for commission.

The church must rise again in Kingdom authority - walking not as beggars but as ambassadors, not as victims but as victors. The King has delegated His authority to a remnant who will not compromise.

154

The Kingdom does not give permission; it gives power. Delegated authority is only as strong as your submission. Calvary was not just about forgiveness - it was about restoration of dominion. Authority unused is authority lost. You cannot rebuke what you secretly entertain. Spiritual authority is not shouting louder - it is standing stronger. Your authority is not in your opinion but in His commission. Authority is not a title; it is a trust.

The remnant must rise - not timidly but triumphantly - walking in Kingdom authority, living as ambassadors of the King.

Scripture Index

- Matthew 28:18
- Luke 10:19
- John 5:19
- James 4:7
- Jeremiah 17:10
- Leviticus 19:16
- 1 Corinthians 6:9–10
- Proverbs 12:22
- John 10:11
- Genesis 1:26–28
- Romans 5:17
- John 19:30

- Matthew 16:19
- Luke 9:1–2
- Acts 3:6–8
- Acts 19:13–16
- John 14:30
- 2 Corinthians 10:4
- Ephesians 6:10–17
- 2 Corinthians 5:20
- John 20:21
- Revelation 4:10
- Acts 1:8

Chapter Sixteen

The Voice of the Bride – A Church in Agreement With the Spirit

Introduction

The greatest sound the earth will ever hear is not the roar of nations or the decrees of kings, but the unified cry of the Spirit and the Bride: *"Come"* (Revelation 22:17). This is the final announcement of history, the ultimate harmony between heaven and earth.

The Bride has no authority if she has no voice. Silence is not humility - it is abdication. The end-time church must rise in holy boldness, finding her voice not in culture, not in politics, not in compromise, but in the Spirit. *"And I John saw the holy city, new Jerusalem, coming down from God out of heaven, prepared as a bride adorned for her husband"* (Revelation 21:2).

The Bride is not silent, nor is she confused. She is clothed in white, her voice purified by fire, her decree aligned with the Spirit. *"He that hath the bride is the bridegroom: but the friend of the bridegroom, which standeth and heareth him, rejoiceth greatly because of the bridegroom's voice"* (John 3:29). The Bride has a voice because she has a Bridegroom.

Ephesians 5:27 declares that Christ is preparing her *"a glorious church, not having spot, or wrinkle, or any such thing; but that it should be holy and without blemish."* Her voice must match her garments - holy, pure, and in agreement with the Spirit.

The Voice That Matches the Spirit

The Spirit's testimony is always of Christ. Jesus said, *"But when the Comforter is come, whom I will send unto you from the Father, even the Spirit of truth, which proceedeth from the Father, he shall testify of me"* (John 15:26). If the Spirit only testifies of Christ, the Bride can speak nothing else.

A divided voice cannot carry a united Kingdom. Two voices cannot call the same Bridegroom. When the church speaks contrary to the Spirit, confusion reigns. But when the church echoes the Spirit's cry, hell trembles, and heaven draws near.

"Can two walk together, except they be agreed?" (Amos 3:3). This is the essence of the Bride's call: agreement. The Spirit and the Bride are in step, in sound, in sync. The Bride's voice is not to be a strange sound mingled with Babylon's noise, but a pure echo of the Spirit.

Revelation closes with the most profound partnership: *"The Spirit and the Bride say, Come"* (Revelation 22:17). Their voices are not in competition but in complete harmony. Authority flows through agreement, and victory is sealed when the Bride's voice mirrors the Spirit's decree.

157

Purity of the Bride's Voice

The purity of the Bride's voice determines the power of her testimony. Paul told the Corinthians, *"I have espoused you to one husband, that I may present you as a chaste virgin to Christ"* (2 Corinthians 11:2). The enemy seeks to corrupt the simplicity of devotion to Christ because compromise always contaminates the voice.

Compromise corrupts the voice; consecration clarifies it. The sound of compromise is static; the sound of consecration is clarity. When the Bride lives divided, her voice carries no weight. When she is consecrated, her sound cuts through the noise.

Psalm 24 asks, *"Who shall ascend into the hill of the Lord? or who shall stand in his holy place? He that hath clean hands, and a pure heart"* (Psalm 24:3–4). Hebrews 12:14 warns, *"Follow peace with all men, and holiness, without which no man shall see the Lord."* Without holiness, the Bride cannot see Him - and if she cannot see Him, she cannot declare Him.

The Bride cannot speak with clarity if her garments are spotted. Her testimony becomes muffled when she mingles with Babylon. But when she is purified by the washing of the Word (Ephesians 5:26), her voice becomes as clear as a trumpet in the earth.

The Authority of Agreement

There is supernatural power in agreement. Jesus said, *"If two of you shall agree on earth as touching anything that they shall ask, it shall be done for them of my Father which is in heaven"* (Matthew 18:19). If the agreement of two carries this much authority, how much greater the agreement of the Spirit and the Bride?

Authority flows where agreement grows. Agreement is not passive - it is prophetic alignment. When two agree in the Spirit, they do not add strength - they multiply it. *"How should one chase a thousand, and two put ten thousand to flight"* (Deuteronomy 32:30)? Agreement produces exponential authority.

Division diminishes authority, but agreement multiplies it. This is why hell's greatest strategy is to fracture the church, but heaven's greatest weapon is to unite her. When the Bride aligns with the Spirit, she carries governmental authority in prayer, worship, and proclamation. Her decrees become heaven's decrees. Her prayers become prophetic summons. She does not beg - she legislates.

The Counterfeit Voices

Wherever heaven speaks, hell counterfeits. False prophets, seducing spirits, and cultural voices attempt to drown out the voice of the Bride. John warned, *"Beloved, believe not every spirit, but try the spirits whether they are of God: because many false prophets are gone out into the world"* (1 John 4:1).

Paul warned of a time when men would "not endure sound doctrine; but after their own lusts shall heap to themselves teachers, having itching ears; and they shall turn away their ears from the truth, and shall be turned unto fables" (2 Timothy 4:3–4).

Hell always tries to imitate what heaven originates. Hell cannot create; it only corrupts. The serpent has always spoken lies to distort the voice of truth. Even Satan himself, Paul said, "is transformed into an angel of light" (2 Corinthians 11:14).

False unity produces noise, not power. Only Spirit-Bride unity produces authority. True unity is never born from submission to the whims of a congregational leader, especially when those whims excuse sin or protect corruption within the body - it is built only on obedience to Christ. Unity that bows to man's will instead of God's Word is deception in disguise. For it is written, *"Can two walk together, except they be agreed?"* (Amos 3:3). Agreement with darkness is not unity - it is rebellion against the Light.

No man is ever to exalt himself in the place of the Father or of Christ. For there is only one God and one Mediator between God and men, the man Christ Jesus (1 Timothy 2:5). Any man who seeks that position invites judgment, for it is written, *"Call no man your father upon the earth: for one is your Father, which is in heaven"* (Matthew 23:9). Authority may guide - but only Christ rules. The

160

Bride must refuse to echo culture's compromise or Babylon's confusion. She must carry the frequency of heaven. Her voice must pierce through deception with the clarity of divine truth.

The Bride's Prophetic Decree

The Bride does not murmur - she prophesies. She does not whisper - she declares. Isaiah said, *"For Zion's sake will I not hold my peace, and for Jerusalem's sake I will not rest, until the righteousness thereof go forth as brightness, and the salvation thereof as a lamp that burneth"* (Isaiah 62:1).

The Bride does not echo earth - she amplifies heaven. Jeremiah testified, *"Then the Lord put forth his hand, and touched my mouth. And the Lord said unto me, Behold, I have put my words in thy mouth. See, I have this day set thee over the nations and over the kingdoms, to root out, and to pull down, and to destroy, and to throw down, to build, and to plant"* (Jeremiah 1:9–10).

The Bride's voice is not ornamental; it is governmental. Her decree shakes nations and awakens generations. *"Let us be glad and rejoice, and give honour to him: for the marriage of the Lamb is come, and his wife hath made herself ready"* (Revelation 19:7). Her readiness is seen not only in her garments but in her voice.

The prophetic voice of the Bride declares, *"The kingdoms of this world are become the kingdoms of our Lord, and of his Christ"* (Revelation 11:15). This is not a suggestion but a decree, a sound that shifts atmospheres and sets captives free.

161

Living in Agreement With the Spirit

Agreement with the Spirit is not theory; it is obedience. Paul declared, *"For as many as are led by the Spirit of God, they are the sons of God"* (Romans 8:14). The true sons and daughters follow His leading, not their own desires.

Agreement is obedience in action. The Spirit leads; the Bride follows. The Spirit speaks; the Bride echoes. Agreement means walking in step with Him. Paul exhorts, *"If we live in the Spirit, let us also walk in the Spirit"* (Galatians 5:25).

This was the testimony of the early church. *"It seemed good to the Holy Ghost, and to us"* (Acts 15:28). Agreement with the Spirit was their measure for decision-making, their compass for direction.

To live in agreement is to surrender personal agendas for Kingdom alignment. It is to silence lesser voices and amplify the Spirit's voice until there is no dissonance between heaven and earth. Agreement is costly, but it is powerful.

Conclusion: The Unified Voice

The final cry of the earth will not come from governments or empires but from the Spirit and the Bride. Together they declare, *"Come"* (Revelation 22:17). This is the voice that summons the King.

The last sound hell will hear is the unified cry of the Spirit and the Bride. Joel 2:16 prophesies: *"Gather the people, sanctify the congregation, assemble the elders, gather the children… let the bridegroom go forth of his chamber, and the bride out of her closet."* The Bride is not hiding; she is emerging with a voice.

The end-time church must carry the same voice as the end-time Spirit. The Spirit says, "Come." The Bride echoes, "Come." Their agreement hastens the return of the Lord.

Isaiah 60:1 declares, *"Arise, shine; for thy light is come, and the glory of the Lord is risen upon thee."* This is the call of the Bride in agreement with the Spirit: to rise, to shine, to declare the glory of the King until He returns.

The Spirit and the Bride do not speak in two voices but in one. And that one voice is summoning the earth to prepare for the coming of the Bridegroom King.

Scripture Index

- 1 Timothy 2:5
- 2 Timothy 4:3–4
- 2 Corinthians 11:14
- Isaiah 62:1
- Jeremiah 1:9–10
- Revelation 19:7–8

- Revelation 11:15
- Romans 8:14
- Galatians 5:25
- Acts 15:28
- Joel 2:16
- Isaiah 60:1

Chapter Seventeen

The End-Time Remnant – A People Prepared for the King

Introduction

In every generation, God preserves a people within a people. A voice within the noise. A flame that refuses to be extinguished. *"And it shall come to pass in that day, that the remnant of Israel… shall stay upon the Lord, the Holy One of Israel, in truth"* (Isaiah 10:20).

The call of the remnant is not to survive but to overcome. They are not content to blend in with Babylon; they are marked by their allegiance to the King. Paul declared, *"Even so then at this present time also there is a remnant according to the election of grace"* (Romans 11:5).

God always preserves a people within a people. When the masses bow, the remnant stands. When compromise spreads, the remnant consecrates. When darkness deepens, the remnant shines brighter. They are a prophetic sign of hope, a people prepared for the King.

"Except the Lord of hosts had left unto us a very small remnant, we should have been as Sodom, and we should have been like unto Gomorrah" (Isaiah 1:9). The remnant is God's evidence that His covenant cannot be broken. Romans 9:27 reminds us, *"Though the number of*

the children of Israel be as the sand of the sea, a remnant shall be saved." The counsel of the Lord stands forever (Psalm 33:11). The remnant is God's proof that His promises cannot die.

The Mark of the Remnant

The remnant is not defined by numbers but by faithfulness. In a world obsessed with crowds, God looks for covenant carriers. Micah prophesied, *"The remnant of Jacob shall be in the midst of many people as a dew from the Lord, as the showers upon the grass"* (Micah 5:7). The remnant is like dew - small, almost unnoticed, but vital to life.

The remnant is small in size but massive in authority. Their strength is not in their multitude but in their mandate. Zephaniah 3:12–13 promises: *"I will also leave in the midst of thee an afflicted and poor people, and they shall trust in the name of the Lord. The remnant of Israel shall not do iniquity, nor speak lies."*

The remnant does not measure success by popularity but by presence. They are not impressed by numbers; they are marked by intimacy with God. Jesus declared, *"Strait is the gate, and narrow is the way, which leadeth unto life, and few there be that find it"* (Matthew 7:14).

God has always worked through remnants: Noah found grace and preserved humanity through obedience. Elijah thought he was alone, but God had reserved 7,000 who had not bowed to

Baal (1 Kings 19:18). Jesus warned, *"He that shall endure unto the end, the same shall be saved"* (Matthew 24:13).

Their mark is purity. Their distinction is truth. They do not manipulate, lie, or compromise. Their yes means yes, their no means no. They are marked not by eloquence but by endurance. Not by appearance but by alignment.

The Purification of the Remnant

The remnant is not chosen for ease but for endurance. They are a people purified by fire. *"And I will bring the third part through the fire, and will refine them as silver is refined, and will try them as gold is tried: they shall call on my name, and I will hear them"* (Zechariah 13:9).

The fire doesn't destroy the remnant - it defines it. Babylon's fire could not consume the three Hebrew boys; it only revealed the fourth man walking with them. Malachi 3:3 declares, *"And he shall sit as a refiner and purifier of silver: and he shall purify the sons of Levi."*

The furnace is the remnant's birthplace. Trials are not punishment but preparation. Peter wrote, *"That the trial of your faith, being much more precious than of gold that perisheth, though it be tried with fire, might be found unto praise and honour and glory at the appearing of Jesus Christ"* (1 Peter 1:7).

Isaiah 48:10 says, *"Behold, I have refined thee, but not with silver; I have chosen thee in the furnace of affliction."* Paul reminds us,

"Tribulation worketh patience; and patience, experience; and experience, hope" (Romans 5:3–4).

God does not trust untested vessels with end-time authority. The fire removes the mixture. The heat reveals the hidden. The process does not weaken - it strengthens. The remnant emerges from refining with eyes fixed, hearts clean, and voices clear.

The Remnant's Separation From Babylon

The remnant's first mark of distinction is separation. They may live in Babylon, but they refuse to bow to it. Daniel *"purposed in his heart that he would not defile himself with the portion of the king's meat"* (Daniel 1:8). Separation is not isolation - it is consecration.

The remnant refuses to feast at Babylon's table. Revelation 18:4 is heaven's command: *"Come out of her, my people, that ye be not partakers of her sins."* The remnant leaves compromise not out of pride but out of pursuit. They know that intimacy with the King demands distance from Babylon.

You cannot walk in Zion while feasting in Babylon. Paul declares, *"Wherefore come out from among them, and be ye separate, saith the Lord, and touch not the unclean thing; and I will receive you"* (2 Corinthians 6:17). Moses himself refused Egypt's treasures: *"By faith Moses, when he was come to years, refused to be called the son of Pharaoh's daughter; choosing rather to suffer affliction with the people of God"* (Hebrews 11:24–26).

Ezra 9:8–9 shows how God granted a remnant a little reviving in their bondage. Paul wrote that in a great house there are vessels of honor and dishonor, and if a man purge himself, he shall be a vessel unto honor (2 Timothy 2:20–21).

Separation is not optional - it is the lifeblood of the remnant. They understand that friendship with the world is enmity with God (James 4:4). Their separation is not to retreat but to represent. They are in Babylon, but Babylon is not in them.

The Authority of the Remnant

The remnant carries authority because they carry alignment. Joel 2:32 declares, *"And it shall come to pass, that whosoever shall call on the name of the Lord shall be delivered: for in mount Zion and in Jerusalem shall be deliverance, and in the remnant whom the Lord shall call."* Deliverance flows through the remnant because they are aligned with Zion.

The remnant carries the roar of Zion in the face of Babylon. They are not timid - they are triumphant. Obadiah 1:17 proclaims, *"But upon mount Zion shall be deliverance, and there shall be holiness; and the house of Jacob shall possess their possessions."*

The roar of the remnant is not volume - it is alignment. Joshua 23:10 promises, *"One man of you shall chase a thousand: for the Lord your God, he it is that fighteth for you."* Authority flows not from performance but from obedience. Authority flows to those who bow lower.

Luke 10:19 confirms the promise: *"Behold, I give unto you power to tread on serpents and scorpions, and over all the power of the enemy."* In Acts 4:13, even the enemies of the Gospel recognized authority when they saw the boldness of Peter and John and *"took knowledge of them, that they had been with Jesus."*

Their authority is not borrowed; it is bestowed. It is not in their name but in His. They carry Kingdom dominion not because of who they are, but because of who they represent. When the remnant speaks, it is as ambassadors of the King, decreeing heaven's word into earth's chaos.

The Assignment of the Remnant

The remnant is not preserved to merely exist - they are preserved to build. Amos 9:11 prophesies, *"In that day will I raise up the tabernacle of David that is fallen, and close up the breaches thereof; and I will raise up his ruins, and I will build it as in the days of old."*

The remnant finishes what history began. They are restorers of altars, rebuilders of ruins, repairers of breaches. Haggai 2:9 declares, *"The glory of this latter house shall be greater than of the former."* The remnant carries that promise, not as a theory but as an assignment.

The remnant does not just survive history - they redeem it. Isaiah 58:12 calls them *"the repairer of the breach, the restorer of paths to dwell in."* Ezekiel 37:10 shows them as an army: *"So I prophesied as he commanded me, and the breath came into them, and they lived, and stood up upon their feet, an exceeding great army."*

Nehemiah declared, *"Ye see the distress that we are in, how Jerusalem lieth waste… come, and let us build up the wall of Jerusalem, that we be no more a reproach"* (Nehemiah 2:17). Isaiah 61:4 prophesies: *"And they shall build the old wastes, they shall raise up the former desolations, and they shall repair the waste cities."*

The remnant rebuilds altars that release fire. Elijah on Mount Carmel restored the altar of the Lord, and fire fell (1 Kings 18:30–39). The assignment of the remnant is apostolic and prophetic: to rebuild what was broken and to call down fire that proves God is God.

The Hope of the Remnant

The remnant does not live in despair - they live in hope. Their vision is fixed not on Babylon's noise but on Zion's promise. *"And they overcame him by the blood of the Lamb, and by the word of their testimony; and they loved not their lives unto the death"* (Revelation 12:11).

The remnant is not hiding - they are heralding. They are not shrinking back - they are pressing forward. Jesus said, *"Fear not, little flock; for it is your Father's good pleasure to give you the kingdom"* (Luke 12:32).

The remnant are hope-carriers in a hopeless world. Their hope is not naive - it is anchored in eternity. *"This I recall to my*

171

mind, therefore have I hope. It is of the Lord's mercies that we are not consumed, because his compassions fail not. They are new every morning" (Lamentations 3:21–23).

Hope is the fuel of endurance. Paul wrote of *"the work of faith, and labour of love, and patience of hope in our Lord Jesus Christ"* (1 Thessalonians 1:3). Hebrews 6:19 declares, *"Which hope we have as an anchor of the soul, both sure and stedfast."* Titus 2:13 calls it *"that blessed hope, and the glorious appearing of the great God and our Saviour Jesus Christ."*

Hope is their anchor. Faith is their compass. Love is their fuel. They live with eternity in their eyes and destiny in their hands. Their hope is not in survival but in revival. Not in escape but in the establishment of the King's reign.

Conclusion: A People Prepared

The remnant is the prophetic sign that God's plan is unstoppable. They are the hinge of history, the evidence of God's covenant faithfulness. Romans 8:19 declares, *"For the earnest expectation of the creature waiteth for the manifestation of the sons of God."* Creation groans for their revealing.

The end-time remnant is the Bride prepared, the army assembled, and the sons revealed. They are lovers and warriors, priests and kings, servants and rulers. They are not defined by their weakness but by His strength.

The remnant is both the womb and the warrior of the end-time harvest. Like John the Baptist, they prepare the way of the Lord: *"And he shall go before him in the spirit and power of Elias, to turn the hearts of the fathers to the children… to make ready a people prepared for the Lord"* (Luke 1:17). They are the wise virgins of Matthew 25, with lamps trimmed and oil burning, awaiting the cry at midnight: *"Behold, the bridegroom cometh."*

Revelation 7:14 describes them as those *"which came out of great tribulation, and have washed their robes, and made them white in the blood of the Lamb."* Hebrews 12:22–24 shows their destiny: *"But ye are come unto mount Sion, and unto the city of the living God… to the general assembly and church of the firstborn."*

Revelation 21:2 shows the end of the story: the Bride prepared, coming down in glory, adorned for her Husband. The remnant becomes the Bride, perfected and ready, summoning the King with one voice: "Come, Lord Jesus."

Scripture Index

- Isaiah 10:20–22
- Romans 11:5
- Isaiah 1:9
- Romans 9:27
- Psalm 33:11
- Micah 5:7–8
- Zephaniah 3:12–13
- Matthew 7:14
- 1 Kings 19:18
- Matthew 24:13
- Zechariah 13:9
- Malachi 3:3

- Isaiah 48:10
- Romans 5:3–4
- 1 Peter 1:7
- Daniel 1:8
- Revelation 18:4
- James 4:4
- 2 Corinthians 6:17
- Hebrews 11:24–26
- Ezra 9:8–9
- 2 Timothy 2:20–21
- Joel 2:32
- Obadiah 1:17
- Joshua 23:10
- Luke 10:19
- Acts 4:13
- Amos 9:11–12
- Haggai 2:6–9

- Isaiah 58:12
- Isaiah 61:4
- Nehemiah 2:17
- 1 Kings 18:30–39
- Ezekiel 37:10
- Revelation 12:11
- Luke 12:32
- Lamentations 3:21–23
- 1 Thessalonians 1:3
- Hebrews 6:19
- Titus 2:13
- Romans 8:19
- Luke 1:17
- Matthew 25:1–13
- Revelation 7:14
- Hebrews 12:22–24
- Revelation 21:2

Chapter Eighteen

Thinking Like a Master Builder

"According to the grace of God which is given unto me, as a wise master builder, I have laid the foundation, and another builds thereon. But let every man take heed how he builds thereupon." (1 Corinthians 3:10)

Introduction: The Call to Build with Wisdom

God never leaves His house to chance. From the earliest days, His pattern has been clear: He raises up builders who construct according to His blueprint, not their own imagination. Noah did not build the ark according to his personal preferences but according to divine instruction (Genesis 6:14–16). Moses did not design the tabernacle based on cultural styles but on what he saw in the heavenly vision (Exodus 25:40). Solomon did not create the temple from scratch but followed the blueprint David received in prayer (1 Chronicles 28:11–12).

In this New Covenant era, the local church is that dwelling place - the ekklesia of God, built on the foundation of apostles and prophets, with Jesus Christ as the Chief Cornerstone (Ephesians 2:20–22). Leaders today are summoned not merely to maintain services but to build enduring structures of transformation. They are called to think, plan, and labor as master builders.

175

The prophetic insight: Milk makes an audience. Meat makes an army. This is the starting point. Churches cannot remain nurseries forever. Leaders cannot keep recycling milk when the hour demands soldiers ready for battle. The Spirit is summoning leaders to think like apostolic builders, constructing with vision, foresight, and eternal weight. The call is urgent: stop entertaining, start building.

Apostolic Oversight: Paul's Model of a Master Builder

Paul's declaration in 1 Corinthians 3:10 cuts through every shallow approach to ministry: *"According to the grace of God which is given unto me, as a wise master builder, I have laid the foundation..."* He does not claim to be a celebrity preacher, a motivational speaker, or a crowd-gatherer. He calls himself a wise master builder.

To be a master builder is to function apostolically. It is to carry God's design for the foundation and ensure others build upon it faithfully. Paul warns: *"But let every man take heed how he builds thereupon."* (1 Corinthians 3:10) The Church is not a playground for man's imagination. It is a construction site where heaven's blueprint must be honored.

Teachers, preachers, and evangelists build on top of the foundations that apostles and prophets lay. It is not the other way around. When that order is reversed, chaos is the result. Apostolic and prophetic oversight is not optional - it is foundational.

This is why Paul draws the contrast between building with gold, silver, precious stones versus wood, hay, and stubble (1 Corinthians 3:12–13). Every ministry, every program, every structure will one day be tested by fire. What was born of flesh will burn; what was born of Spirit will remain. Apostolic leaders live with that judgment in mind.

The General Contractor of the Kingdom

The analogy of a general contractor is not accidental. A contractor does not hammer every nail or carry every stone. His responsibility is to see the big picture, to coordinate the labor, to ensure the design is honored. Apostolic leaders must function in the same way.

Many churches stall because the senior leader has confused their role. Instead of functioning as an overseer of the blueprint, they function as an exhausted laborer doing everyone else's job. The sobering truth is this: the church will only grow to the point where a leader's incompetence exceeds their ability. That is the ceiling every leader faces when they refuse to rise into oversight and insist on doing it all themselves.

This is the essence of what is often called the Peter Principle: people rise to the level of their incompetence. Many leaders are promoted or elevated until they reach a point where their skills are insufficient, and from there, decline begins. In the Kingdom, this happens when leaders refuse to release, refuse to delegate, and insist on controlling everything. Their incompetence becomes the lid that halts the expansion of God's house.

Layered upon this is the danger described in the Dunning-Kruger effect: those who are most incompetent often believe themselves to be the most brilliant. They reach erroneous conclusions and make destructive decisions, all while their very incompetence blinds them from recognizing their own ineptitude. In short, the most inept tend to be the most confident in their brilliance. On the other hand, those who are truly wise often underestimate themselves, walking in humility rather than presumption.

Is this not exactly what we see in Saul, the king of Israel? He disobeyed God, presumed he knew better, and yet defended his actions with arrogant confidence (1 Samuel 15:13–23). He was blind to his incompetence, convinced of his greatness, and as a result, he lost the kingdom. Contrast this with Moses, who felt unqualified, slow of speech, and hesitant to lead (Exodus 4:10–12). Yet God chose him because humility made room for grace.

The lesson is clear: the church cannot be led by arrogant incompetence disguised as confidence. Neither can it be overseen by insecure micromanagement that refuses to release others. Master builders must resist both traps. They must recognize that oversight requires wisdom, humility, and vision - functioning not as laborers trapped in the ditch but as contractors overseeing the whole site.

Delegation vs. Micromanagement

This distinction is critical: deacons handle the practical, bishops discern the spiritual, and apostles set the foundation. Confusion arises when leaders blur these roles. A leader who insists on micromanaging every task becomes a bottleneck, stifling growth.

If you cannot see over in the Spirit, you cannot be over in the natural. Oversight requires sight. Leaders who spend all their energy micromanaging details lose the capacity to discern heaven's blueprint. They trade spiritual authority for managerial control.

Delegation multiplies the house; micromanagement strangles it. Paul instructed Timothy not just to teach but to entrust what he heard to faithful men who shall be able to teach others also (2 Timothy 2:2). Apostolic leaders reproduce themselves by releasing others into function. Those who refuse to release will eventually collapse under the weight of control.

Authority is not for manipulation or for testing men - that is God's job. Authority is not for gossip collection or for keeping records of whispered lies to be used later against the sheep. Such behavior is predatory, not pastoral. Scripture warns us: *"A gossip betrays a confidence; so avoid anyone who talks too much"* (Proverbs 20:19). Predatory use of authority is illegal, immoral, and demonic. Master builders are not predators - they are protectors.

Many years ago, before being sent on a new assignment, I had a prophetic dream that lasted as though years of life were compressed into hours. In the dream, I was entrusted with words for a pastor whose destiny was linked to the people of his church. But with that assignment came a warning. I saw rabbits moving everywhere - watching, listening, and spreading gossip. They carried themselves like messengers, reporting everything back to the senior pastor. But what they carried was poisoned. What they delivered was not truth but distortion, manipulated by a lying spirit.

These rabbits were not harmless creatures. Many bore military rank in the dream, meaning they carried authority within the house, and yet their true loyalty was compromised. They funneled "intelligence" back to the general - the senior pastor - but it was corrupted, controlled by deception. Over time, these records accumulated and became weapons against the very flock they were meant to serve.

I was warned: "Watch for the predatory HR practices." These were systems that disguised themselves as accountability but were actually predatory surveillance, storing information to be used against God's people. In the dream, I grew weary of their games, and at times I would deliberately let them overhear conversations, exposing their schemes for what they were and tracking their movements. But the instruction was firm: I was not permitted to kill the rabbits. Only track them and find them, then reveal the situation to the senior pastor at the right time. And then, only when the senior pastor himself gave the order could they be removed.

Each rabbit represented a lying and gossiping spirit. Their colors and fur spoke of the families and groups they were aligned with. The rabbits did not merely repeat what they overheard; they added to it, twisting truth, and then cloaking it in spiritual language - claiming prophetic insight or discernment to give their lies weight. Meanwhile, the garden of the Lord - the church itself - was being devoured. These spirits ate at the pastor's field (the garden), robbing him of the very people God had sent as doors into his destiny.

For destiny is not tied to the monuments you build, but to the people who walk through the doors God assigns to your care. In dreams, people often represent doors, because each person can open access to regions of destiny and inheritance (Revelation 3:20). When gossip and lying spirits devour those people, they devour the future of the church.

This is why gossip and micromanagement are not harmless habits but lethal poisons. They consume the prophetic garden, rob leaders of the voices they need, and strip the church of the destiny God ordained. Rabbits must be exposed. Lying spirits must be discerned. And leaders must guard against any system that replaces trust, testimony, and transparency with surveillance, suspicion, and slander.

Rabbits attract predators - snakes, foxes, and every kind of devourer - and there is far more to this dream than can be fully revealed here. The senior pastor in that dream once had a destiny to have a congregation of over fifteen thousand souls. Heaven had outlined assignments beyond his imagination; glimpses were shown, invitations were extended, and time after time, the Lord gave opportunities to step into it, including the realm where the gifts flowed. Even his life was prolonged by mercy, yet the test kept repeating. Each time meant to refine, not destroy - to draw faith out of delay.

But the prophetic words and teachings he has been waiting to hear, that catalyst for his fire, will not appear until he moves in obedience. Heaven has already spoken; now faith must answer. His private tests concealed the very key he sought, and his hesitation has only extended the season. Still, the grace of God lingers - there is a window of mercy left open. Many leaders stand in this same place, between unfulfilled prophecy and unfinished obedience. Yet the Spirit whispers even now: There is still hope of calling. For as long as breath remains, restoration is possible. The story of Samson still declares it - strength can return, purpose can rise again, and destiny can be rebuilt. This was not the first time I have seen a man with a similar call for a particular region. This is the fourth for the same region, and another has started to grow.

(For a deeper prophetic study on hope and restoration, see the book entitled The Unique Factor (Webb, 2025) - the section on Samson's renewal.)

Vision is the Framework

Proverbs 29:18 declares: *"Where there is no vision, the people perish."* Vision is the framework of all construction. Without it, materials pile up aimlessly. With it, every resource finds its place.

Truth must always carry context, content, and conclusion. Without context, truth dies with one generation. Without content, it starves the hearer. Without conclusion, it remains unfinished and ineffective.

Paul modeled this. He communicated with clarity, painting the blueprint again and again until the people saw themselves in it. Apostolic leaders must do the same. They cannot assume people know the vision - they must repeat it, declare it, and embody it until it becomes culture.

Vision is more than a statement on a wall. Vision is the Spirit-breathed framework of the house. It explains why sacrifices are made, why delays are endured, and why unity must be guarded. Without vision, churches fracture into factions. With vision, they march as an army.

The Limits of Leadership Competence

The truth remains: the church will only grow to the point where incompetence exceeds ability. This is not condemnation but calibration. Every leader has a ceiling, a point at which their refusal to grow, release, or discern halts the expansion of the house.

Saul capped the nation's destiny through his insecurity and disobedience (1 Samuel 15:23). Eli capped the priesthood through his refusal to discipline his sons (1 Samuel 2:29). Even Moses, who saw God face to face, reached a ceiling when he struck the rock in anger instead of obeying God's word (Numbers 20:12).

God's people will always rise higher than the ceiling of their leader's maturity, or they will scatter to find a builder who can carry them higher. Leaders must face this truth: either competence expands through grace, humility, and delegation, or incompetence becomes the lid over God's people. Master builders are not perfect, but they are teachable. They seek counsel, they release authority, and they refuse to let pride trap them in a ceiling of decline.

Building by Grace, Not Flesh

Paul anchors everything in grace: *"According to the grace of God which is given unto me…"* (1 Corinthians 3:10). Grace is not a theological concept; it is divine enablement to build what human strength cannot.

Psalm 127:1 echoes this: *"Except the Lord build the house, they labor in vain that build it."* Ministries built on charisma, marketing, or human ingenuity may look impressive for a season, but they collapse when storms come. Only what grace births will endure.

Advertising may catch people, but it cannot keep them. They are not coming to be entertained; they are coming to be transformed. If you build without God, you build in vain. Leaders who run ahead of the Spirit, driven by ambition instead of revelation, may gather crowds but they will never build God's house. Master builders remain in conversation with the Master Builder. They do not presume; they receive. They do not invent; they obey.

Raising Builders, Not Consumers

Jesus did not gather an audience; He raised builders. He called fishermen and turned them into apostles. He called tax collectors and turned them into evangelists. His method was not classroom lectures but apprenticeships - watch, follow, do.

Leadership that works hard but reproduces nothing is sterile. A mule is strong but barren. The mule can carry heavy loads, but it will never multiply. Churches filled with mule-leaders will work hard but leave no legacy. Apostolic leadership cannot afford sterility. Leaders must multiply themselves by raising others to build.

Paul's charge to Timothy was generational: entrust what you've received to faithful men who will teach others (2 Timothy 2:2). This is four generations of builders in one verse. That is the apostolic standard. Leaders who hoard authority die with their work. Leaders who raise builders create a legacy that outlives them.

Accountability on Judgment Day

Paul's warning resounds: *"Let every man take heed how he builds…"* (1 Corinthians 3:10). One day, fire will test the work. This is not metaphorical - it is eternal reality.

If you cannot give your transparent testimony, you are disqualified from building. Testimony is not optional; it is spiritual food. Without it, leaders starve the next generation. Revelation 12:11 thunders: *"They overcame him by the blood of the Lamb, and by the word of their testimony."*

On that day, applause will not matter. Titles will not matter. Size will not matter. Only substance will remain. Wood, hay, and stubble will vanish; gold, silver, and precious stones will endure. Leaders who manipulated, gossiped, or abused authority will see their works consumed in fire. Leaders who built faithfully, humbly, and transparently will see eternal reward.

Builders do not *expand* God's throne; they *express* it. The Kingdom is already established; our obedience simply makes its reality visible in our cities and families.

Conclusion: Building with Eternity in View

To think like a master builder is to build with eternity in view. Apostolic leaders labor not for applause but for permanence. They measure success not by crowds but by construction. They do not ask, "How many came?" but "What was built?"

The work defines the man. Elder is the nature; bishop is the function. Titles without fruit mean nothing. What matters is whether the house was built in alignment with Christ, the Chief Cornerstone.

The Spirit is calling forth a generation of Nehemiahs who will rise and rebuild the broken walls, leaders who will oversee construction until the house of God stands as a holy habitation in the Spirit. They will reject manipulation, gossip, and micromanagement. They will raise builders, not consumers. They will build with grace, not flesh.

And the trumpet call echoes one more time: Milk makes an audience. Meat makes an army. The days of shallow entertainment are over. The days of wise master builders are here.

The foundation is Christ. The blueprint is His Word. The grace is available. The fire is coming. The call is clear: Build as a wise master builder.

Scripture Index

Chapter Nineteen

Teamwork in the Spirit – Synergy, Avoiding Comparison, and Shared Labor

Introduction: The Kingdom Requires Unity

The Kingdom of God has never been advanced by solitary personalities or lone rangers standing apart from the body. It has always been a collective story of a people joined in covenant, empowered by the Spirit, and moving in divine synergy. The church was never designed to be built on the charisma of a single leader, but on the cooperation of many members working in harmony.

Paul declared this Kingdom principle: *"For we are labourers together with God: ye are God's husbandry, ye are God's building"* (1 Corinthians 3:9). Notice the power of the phrase *"together with God."* We are not merely laborers for God as hired servants, but laborers with God as sons and daughters carrying His authority and heart into the earth.

You cannot build the Kingdom alone. The days of lone rangers are over. God never asked one man to carry His Kingdom - He asked a body.

God never builds monuments to men; He builds families that become armies. The Kingdom is not one man with a microphone; it's a body moving as one.

189

Scripture confirms this blueprint. *"From whom the whole body fitly joined together and compacted by that which every joint supplieth... maketh increase of the body unto the edifying of itself in love"* (Ephesians 4:16). And the psalmist declared: *"Behold, how good and how pleasant it is for brethren to dwell together in unity! ... for there the LORD commanded the blessing"* (Psalm 133:1,3). Unity is the atmosphere where God commands blessing and releases His power.

Even Jesus, in His final priestly prayer, revealed that the witness of the Church to the world hinges on unity: *"That they all may be one; as thou, Father, art in me, and I in thee, that they also may be one in us: that the world may believe that thou hast sent me"* (John 17:21).

The Kingdom requires unity because the Kingdom is a body, not a crowd. It is an army, not an audience.

Laborers Together with God

Paul illustrated this principle of shared Kingdom labor: *"I have planted, Apollos watered; but God gave the increase"* (1 Corinthians 3:6). One planted, another watered, but both depended on God for increase. Neither could claim supremacy. *"So then neither is he that planteth any thing, neither he that watereth; but God that giveth the increase"* (1 Corinthians 3:7).

The nursery worker who holds a baby so a mother can hear the gospel is as much a laborer in that soul's salvation as the preacher who gives the altar call.

If you don't see yourself as a laborer, you'll slip into being a spectator. The platform is not the only place God measures; He measures faithfulness in every place.

Jesus taught this principle in John 4:36–37: *"He that reapeth receiveth wages, and gathereth fruit unto life eternal: that both he that soweth and he that reapeth may rejoice together."*

"And whatsoever ye do, do it heartily, as to the Lord, and not unto men; knowing that of the Lord ye shall receive the reward of the inheritance" (Colossians 3:23–24). *"Let us not be weary in well doing: for in due season we shall reap, if we faint not"* (Galatians 6:9).

The Kingdom increases only where there is cooperation. If the planter despises the waterer, or the waterer envies the planter, the harvest is hindered. But when every role is honored, God releases supernatural increase.

The Cancer of Comparison

Paul warned: *"For we dare not make ourselves of the number, or compare ourselves with some that commend themselves: but they measuring themselves by themselves, and comparing themselves among themselves, are not wise"* (2 Corinthians 10:12).

Comparison is cancer. Either you'll get puffed up with pride, or you'll shrink back in shame. Both kill fruitfulness.

Comparison is the devil's counterfeit for discernment. If you're looking left and right, you'll never move forward in

191

Kingdom purpose. Jealousy is proof you've forgotten your own assignment.

James wrote, *"For where envying and strife is, there is confusion and every evil work"* (James 3:16). Solomon said, *"A sound heart is the life of the flesh: but envy the rottenness of the bones"* (Proverbs 14:30).

Paul asked: *"If the whole body were an eye, where were the hearing? If the whole were hearing, where were the smelling?"* (1 Corinthians 12:17). Every part is essential. *"The eye cannot say to the hand, I have no need of thee"* (1 Corinthians 12:21).

Comparison fractures churches. It breeds jealousy among leaders, discouragement among members, and division among ministries. But when honor replaces comparison, the body thrives.

Synergy in the Spirit

Paul used the Greek word sunergos in 1 Corinthians 3:9 - meaning "fellow worker" or "co-laborer." Sunergos is the Greek word from which the English word synergy was derived. Synergy is more than cooperation; it is multiplication. It is when the combined effect of God's people laboring together far exceeds what they could accomplish individually.

"One shall chase a thousand, and two put ten thousand to flight" (Deuteronomy 32:30). *"If two of you shall agree on earth as touching anything that they shall ask, it shall be done for them of my Father which is in heaven"* (Matthew 18:19).

Synergy is heaven's math. It is not $1 + 1 = 2$. It is $1 + 1 = 10,000$.

One voice can shake a room; a united voice can shake a city. Demons scatter when believers stop competing and start completing each other.

Paul exhorted: *"Stand fast in one spirit, with one mind striving together for the faith of the gospel"* (Philippians 1:27). *"Can two walk together, except they be agreed?"* (Amos 3:3).

Abram's 318 trained servants (Genesis 14:14) defeated five kings through synergy. The apostles, once fishermen and tax collectors, turned the world upside down (Acts 17:6) when they labored together under the Spirit's power.

One person with a vision is powerful. A team with the same vision is unstoppable.

Prophetic warning: Unity is not uniformity; it is Spirit-forged harmony across diverse gifts (1 Corinthians 12). True synergy never erases individuality; it weaves it together for Kingdom purpose.

Shared Labor, Shared Reward

Jesus taught: *"When thou doest alms, let not thy left hand know what thy right hand doeth: that thine alms may be in secret: and thy Father which seeth in secret himself shall reward thee openly"* (Matthew 6:3–4).

Paul wrote: *"Every man shall receive his own reward according to his own labour"* (1 Corinthians 3:8).

Heaven pays by faithfulness, not by fame. If you're faithful in the hidden place, you'll shine in the eternal place. Heaven does not separate the pulpit from the pew; heaven sees one harvest field. If you held the rope while others climbed, you are part of the summit. The one unseen on earth may be the most celebrated in heaven.

"For God is not unrighteous to forget your work and labour of love" (Hebrews 6:10). Jesus promised: *"Well done, thou good and faithful servant... enter thou into the joy of thy lord"* (Matthew 25:21).

The Kingdom is a covenant, not a contest. Every contribution is indispensable.

Practical Application: Building a Team Church

1. Honor Every Role – *"Those members of the body, which seem to be more feeble, are necessary"* (1 Corinthians 12:22).
2. Reject Competition – *"He that planteth and he that watereth are one"* (1 Corinthians 3:8).
3. Train Apprentices, Not Audiences – *"Commit thou to faithful men, who shall be able to teach others also"* (2 Timothy 2:2).
4. Value the Intangibles – unseen things like mercy and prayer sustain the church.
5. Guard Against Division – *"Be kindly affectioned one to another with brotherly love; in honour preferring one another"* (Romans 12:10).
6. Live Relationally – *"Feed the flock of God... not as being lords over God's heritage, but being examples to the flock"* (1 Peter 5:2–3).

7. Reproduce Yourself – Ministry must outlive you.

If your ministry dies with you, you failed. A Kingdom work must outlive you. A real leader is measured not by how many follow him, but by how many he raises to lead. Stop asking, "Who is in charge?"; start asking, "How can we move in step?" The church does not need celebrities; it needs servants with synergy.

The Prophetic Warning to Builders Who Play Games with Promotion

If you play games in promoting people, hear this prophetic warning I have delivered to international corporations and ministries alike: when your decisions drive away a strategic person - someone sent to strengthen your foundation - you have chosen ignorance over wisdom. If your pride causes a trained, covenant-minded individual to walk away, understand what you have done: you have armed your competitor with revelation that was meant to remain within your walls.

Do you really want to compete with one who now carries your blueprints because you let pride guide your promotion? You will lose every time. You will lose the person, and the oil they carried will depart with them. And when they leave, others will follow - for sheep recognize when the shepherd's discernment has died.

If you exalt the second best instead of the best, that is exactly what you will inherit: mediocrity. You may keep your title,

195

but you will forfeit your destiny. Believing that people are easily replaceable is ignorance in any organization - but in ministry, it is rebellion against divine order.

Every person sent to your house was sent for a reason. The one whose gifting you do not understand was sent to strengthen the area where you are weak, or to multiply what you could not multiply alone. Rejecting them is rejecting the provision of heaven.

I have seen ministers weep when those individuals left - confused that someone who only "sang in the choir" became a leader in another church. But the truth is painful: they could not be developed where they were, because leadership could not see past personal bias or the opinions of others. They lost not because the person was rebellious, but because the leader failed to operate with the heart of a father.

When fathers fail to recognize sons, God relocates those sons. And when those sons find another house, even a smaller one, they flourish - because the environment matches their calling. Destiny does not require size; it requires alignment.

If you cannot express your gifting or your call, depression will soon follow. Many spiritual orphans were created by bad fathers who mistook control for care. These are the leaders who crush destiny while pretending to protect the house. And yes, sometimes a person's ambition outruns their maturity, but time will always expose that. Growth reveals truth - because where there is no fruit, there was never a true calling.

Understand this: church congregations are not competitors. Yet sin still moves among them, disguised as wisdom, disguised as caution.

If the Lord sends senior leaders to your congregation - people already carrying oil and capacity - and you do not prepare to send them out to plant, then you have missed your moment of multiplication. I have seen churches that could have birthed ten new houses in a single year but failed to see the opportunity. The father was offended when one left to pioneer, never realizing that heaven had been urging him to release that very thing.

The Lord says: *You cannot trap callings and anointings like prisoners in your house.* When they cannot flow, they will explode. And when they explode, you will call it rebellion - but heaven will call it release.

The rebellion you fear may be the harvest of your own disobedience. Leaders who suppress destiny create the very division they dread. Then they play the victim while refusing to look in the mirror of discernment.

The apostolic pattern is simple: when God sends leaders to you, you train them, bless them, and send them out. That is how the Kingdom multiplies. Jesus never built a cage for His disciples - He built a catapult. He said, "Go into all the world." The command was not to gather indefinitely, but to reproduce.

The Kingdom does not grow by hoarding sons; it grows by sending them. The church that fears losing people will lose the presence of God. But the church that sends people will never lack sons to train.

So, builder of the Kingdom, hear this word: stop playing games with promotion. Stop promoting to punish, and stop demoting to control. Stop confusing favoritism with discernment. The oil runs down the beard of Aaron - it flows from true alignment, not politics.

If you play with oil, you will spill it. If you hoard gifts, you will lose them. And if you silence those whom God sent to multiply you, their absence will become your judgment.

Train them. Trust them. Release them. For Jesus already showed us how - *follow the pattern He gave.*

Conclusion: A Call to Spirit-Empowered Teamwork

The Spirit is summoning the Church into a new dimension of synergy. The era of isolated ministries and personality cults is over. The harvest is too great, the battles too fierce, and the stakes too high.

Imagine a generation walking in divine synergy, where the Spirit multiplies their efforts beyond human capacity. Jesus prayed, *"That they all may be one… that the world may believe that thou hast sent me"* (John 17:21).

At Pentecost, *"they were all with one accord in one place. And suddenly there came a sound from heaven as of a rushing mighty wind"* (Acts

2:1–2). Unity opens the heavens. *"A threefold cord is not quickly broken"* (Ecclesiastes 4:12).

The devil fears one church in unity more than a thousand churches in competition. We will finish the work only if we finish it together.

Scripture Index

- Genesis 2:18
- Genesis 14:14
- Psalm 133:1–3
- Proverbs 14:30
- Ecclesiastes 4:12
- Matthew 6:3–4
- Matthew 18:19
- Matthew 25:21
- Mark 6:7
- John 4:36–37
- John 17:21
- Acts 2:1–2
- Acts 17:6
- Romans 12:10
- 1 Corinthians 12
- 1 Corinthians 3:6–9
- 1 Corinthians 12:17
- 1 Corinthians 12:21–22
- 2 Corinthians 10:12
- Galatians 6:9
- Ephesians 4:16
- Philippians 1:27
- Colossians 3:23–24
- 1 Peter 5:2–3
- James 3:16
- Hebrews 6:10
- Amos 3:3
- Deuteronomy 32:30

Chapter Twenty

Context, Content, Conclusion – Communicating Truth Across Generations

Introduction: Why Communication Matters in the Kingdom

The Kingdom of God has always advanced through communication. Heaven speaks, and history shifts. Creation itself began with a word: *"And God said, Let there be light: and there was light"* (Genesis 1:3). From Moses at Sinai, to the prophets thundering in Israel's streets, to Jesus proclaiming the Sermon on the Mount, God has always moved His people forward through truth proclaimed with power.

Paul revealed this mystery in 1 Corinthians 2:13–14: *"Which things also we speak, not in the words which man's wisdom teacheth, but which the Holy Ghost teacheth; comparing spiritual things with spiritual. But the natural man receiveth not the things of the Spirit of God: for they are foolishness unto him: neither can he know them, because they are spiritually discerned."*

This means spiritual truth cannot be delivered through natural eloquence alone. The Spirit must breathe on our words. A sermon may charm the ear, but only the Spirit can cut to the heart. Teaching without the Spirit is like giving bread with no life in it - it fills the stomach but not the soul.

The world is drowning in information but starving for revelation. Sound bites and slogans echo endlessly, but few words carry eternal weight. The Church cannot afford to mimic the culture's shallow communication. Amos 3:8 says, *"The lion hath roared, who will not fear? the Lord GOD hath spoken, who can but prophesy?"* The roar of God demands proclamation, not commentary.

We must rise as voices that carry context, content, and conclusion - the three pillars of Kingdom communication that make truth receivable, powerful, and actionable. For *"faith cometh by hearing, and hearing by the word of God"* (Romans 10:17). Without Spirit-filled voices, faith cannot be born. Without clear communication, truth cannot cross the generational divide.

Context: Building a Framework for Truth

Context is the frame that allows truth to be understood and applied. Without context, truth becomes abstract, misused, or dismissed. Jesus always gave context before content. His parables drew from everyday life - vineyards, shepherds, nets, coins - so that eternal truth could be anchored in the soil of people's reality. If you give people truth without context, you're handing them a sword with no handle. They will cut themselves and others. Context is the handle that makes truth usable.

Paul modeled this when he wrote: *"I am made all things to all men, that I might by all means save some"* (1 Corinthians 9:22). He never diluted truth, but he gave it in the language people understood. Context is not compromise - it is clarity.

Even Ezra, when he read the Law to Israel, provided context. Nehemiah 8:8 says: *"So they read in the book in the law of God distinctly, and gave the sense, and caused them to understand the reading."* Context ensures understanding.

If you're speaking to spiritual people, context is often implied. But when addressing non-spiritual people, context must be created. Jesus Himself said, *"I have yet many things to say unto you, but ye cannot bear them now"* (John 16:12). Context determines what can be received.

Paul did the same at Mars Hill: *"As I passed by, and beheld your devotions, I found an altar with this inscription, TO THE UNKNOWN GOD. Whom therefore ye ignorantly worship, him declare I unto you"* (Acts 17:23). He built a bridge of context before declaring Christ.

Illustration of Context, Content, and Conclusion:

Consider this: a rabbi, a Catholic priest, and a Pentecostal preacher were traveling together on an airplane. Midway through the flight, the engines began to fail, and the pilot announced that in order to save the plane, everyone would have to lighten the load by confessing their greatest secret before parachuting out.

The rabbi stood up first and said, "I must confess - I sometimes eat pork." The crowd gasped, but nodded in understanding as he prepared to jump.

Next, the Catholic priest rose and said, "I must confess - I sometimes struggle with doubt." The people murmured in shock, but they let him go.

Finally, the Pentecostal preacher stood. He hesitated, cleared his throat, and said, "I must confess - I'm the one who has been gossiping about all of you."

Everyone on the plane gasped, because suddenly the context, the characters, and the conclusion came together with clarity. The humor works because the context (the airplane emergency) is familiar, the content (the identities of the rabbi, priest, and preacher) is recognizable, and the conclusion lands the punchline in a way everyone understands.

This simple story illustrates how powerful communication always rests on those three elements - context, content, and conclusion. Without context, the story makes no sense. Without content, the story has no weight. Without conclusion, the story has no impact.

And here lies the challenge for the modern Church: many people under 35 have no biblical context. They know cultural symbols - golden arches mean McDonald's, Hershey's means chocolate, IBM means computers, Nike's swoosh means sports, Apple's logo means technology - but they have no framework for the Kingdom. When they hear words like covenant, righteousness, or repentance, they draw a blank.

We have two generations now who don't know the Bible, and most sermons assume knowledge that simply isn't there. That is why we must create context if truth is to be received. Truth without context becomes legalism; truth with context becomes transformation.

Content: Spirit-Breathed Truth, Not Human Wisdom

If context is the frame, content is the picture itself. The content of our communication must never be man's speculation or cultural wisdom, but the eternal Word of God empowered by the Spirit.

Paul said: *"Which things also we speak, not in the words which man's wisdom teacheth, but which the Holy Ghost teacheth"* (1 Corinthians 2:13). He reinforced: *"My speech and my preaching was not with enticing words of man's wisdom, but in demonstration of the Spirit and of power"* (1 Corinthians 2:4).

The Holy Spirit is not an afterthought to preaching; He is the preacher. And information without impartation leads to stagnation. Only Spirit-filled content brings transformation.

Jesus confirmed this: *"The words that I speak unto you, they are spirit, and they are life"* (John 6:63). Hebrews 4:12 adds: *"For the word of God is quick, and powerful, and sharper than any twoedged sword… a discerner of the thoughts and intents of the heart."*

Jeremiah testified: *"His word was in mine heart as a burning fire shut up in my bones"* (Jeremiah 20:9). That is Spirit-filled content. Not fluff, not human rhetoric, but fire.

Prophetic insight: Preaching without the Spirit is like reading a love letter in a language you cannot understand: The words are there, the ink is real, but the meaning is lost until the Spirit breathes on it.

Isaiah 55:11 promises: *"So shall my word be that goeth forth out of my mouth: it shall not return unto me void, but it shall accomplish that which I please."* Spirit-breathed content always produces fruit.

The Church is not starving for more content. It is starving for the Spirit. Sermons filled with clever quotes but no fire are sermons that leave people hungry.

Finishing with Clarity and Authority

Every Kingdom message must end with a conclusion that demands a response. Without a conclusion, truth is left as a theory. With conclusion, truth becomes destiny.

Another prophetic insight: A Kingdom conclusion doesn't leave people clapping; it leaves them choosing.

Jesus always concluded with clarity. After teaching on the wise and foolish builders, He said: *"Whosoever heareth these sayings of mine, and doeth them, I will liken him unto a wise man, which built his house upon a rock"* (Matthew 7:24).

Moses concluded the law with choice: *"I have set before you life and death, blessing and cursing: therefore choose life"* (Deuteronomy 30:19). Joshua concluded his leadership with a challenge: *"Choose you this day whom ye will serve... but as for me and my house, we will serve the LORD"* (Joshua 24:15).

At Pentecost, Peter's sermon concluded with a command: *"Repent, and be baptized every one of you in the name of Jesus Christ for the remission of sins"* (Acts 2:38). The result? Three thousand souls were added to the church.

Hebrews 4:7 exhorts: *"Today if ye will hear his voice, harden not your hearts."* A sermon without a conclusion leaves people entertained but unchanged.

Paul's confrontation with Agrippa demonstrates this. After Paul's testimony, Agrippa declared, *"Almost thou persuadest me to be a Christian"* (Acts 26:28). That is the power of a Kingdom conclusion - it forces a choice.

Prophetic Insight: Voices for the Generations

God is raising prophetic voices that will carry truth across generational divides. They will speak with wisdom to elders, clarity to the young, and conviction to the lost.

This prophetic insight thunders if you understand it: We don't need echo chambers; we need trumpets. A trumpet is clear, sharp, and cannot be ignored.

Acts 2:6 shows the miracle at Pentecost: *"Every man heard them speak in his own language."* God ensured the gospel was multilingual and multi-generational from the beginning.

Joel 2:28 prophesies: *"Your sons and your daughters shall prophesy, your old men shall dream dreams, your young men shall see visions."* Truth must move through every age group if it is to advance.

Joel 1:3 commands: *"Tell ye your children of it, and let your children tell their children, and their children another generation."* The Word must be handed off like a torch, never dropped.

Revelatory insight: If we fail to give clear context, our children will grow up Biblically illiterate - and Babylon will teach them its lies.

Practical Application: Teaching Across Generations

1. Build Context Without Compromise. Relate truth in a way people can understand without diluting it (1 Corinthians 9:22; Nehemiah 8:8; Acts 17:23).

2. Preach Spirit-Filled Content. *"All scripture is given by inspiration of God"* (2 Timothy 3:16). Every word must be Spirit-breathed.

3. Conclude With a Call. Always bring people to a decision: *"Choose life"* (Deuteronomy 30:19); *"Repent and be baptized"* (Acts 2:38); *"Harden not your hearts"* (Hebrews 4:7).

4. Equip the Faithful. *"Commit thou to faithful men, who shall be able to teach others also"* (2 Timothy 2:2). Faithful people multiply truth; unfaithful people bury it. Jesus echoed this in Matthew

7:6: *"Give not that which is holy unto the dogs, neither cast ye your pearls before swine."*

5. Guard Against Dilution. Do not replace eternal truth with cultural slogans. Jesus said, *"Heaven and earth shall pass away, but my words shall not pass away"* (Matthew 24:35).

6. Teach With Fire. Let the Word burn before you speak. Jeremiah 20:9 reminds us: the Word must be like fire shut up in your bones. If you train spectators, you will get applause; if you train soldiers, you will get a harvest.

> Context without Spirit is confusion.
> Content without Spirit is dead.
> Conclusion without Spirit is empty.
> But Spirit in all three is transformation.

Conclusion: Rising as Communicators of Kingdom Truth

The future of the Church depends on its communication. Without context, truth is misunderstood. Without Spirit-filled content, truth is powerless. Without conclusion, truth is unfinished.

Context makes truth receivable. Content makes truth powerful. Conclusion makes truth actionable.

We are not entertainers but ambassadors (2 Corinthians 5:20). We are not commentators but heralds (Romans 10:14–15).

God has entrusted us with words that shift nations, awaken generations, and prepare the Bride for the return of the King.

Revelation 19:10 declares: *"For the testimony of Jesus is the spirit of prophecy."* That is the ultimate aim of Spirit-filled communication - to point to Jesus, testify of His Kingdom, and call all generations to obedience.

One final prophetic charge resounds: Words are weapons; wield them with precision. Every generation is shaped by the voices it listens to - make sure yours is a trumpet for the Kingdom.

Scripture Index

- Genesis 1:3
- Nehemiah 8:8
- Jeremiah 20:9
- Isaiah 55:11
- Matthew 7:24
- Matthew 24:35
- Matthew 7:6
- John 6:63
- John 16:12
- Acts 2:6
- Acts 2:38
- Acts 17:23
- Acts 26:28

- Romans 10:14–15
- Romans 10:17
- 1 Corinthians 2:4
- 1 Corinthians 2:13–14
- 1 Corinthians 9:22
- 2 Corinthians 5:20
- 2 Timothy 2:2
- 2 Timothy 3:16
- Deuteronomy 30:19
- Joshua 24:15
- Joel 1:3
- Joel 2:28
- Hebrews 4:7

- Hebrews 4:12
- Revelation 19:10
- Amos 3:8

Chapter Twenty-One

Apostolic Leadership – Order, Authority, and Fathering

Introduction: Apostolic Foundations

The Church of Jesus Christ was never meant to be built on programs, personalities, or popularity. It was designed to be built on the foundation of apostles and prophets, with Christ Jesus Himself as the chief cornerstone (Ephesians 2:20). Apostolic leadership is not a luxury - it is a necessity. Without it, churches drift into disorder, fragmentation, and weakness.

Paul declared that Christ gave apostles, prophets, evangelists, pastors, and teachers *"for the perfecting of the saints, for the work of the ministry, for the edifying of the body of Christ"* (Ephesians 4:11–12). Apostles are not celebrities - they are master builders (1 Corinthians 3:10). They are not hirelings - they are fathers who reproduce sons.

A prophetic warning has been sounded: Without apostolic order, churches become noisy but powerless. Apostolic fathers bring alignment that attracts heaven.

Malachi 4:5–6 declared the end-time restoration: *"He shall turn the heart of the fathers to the children, and the heart of the children to their fathers."* Apostolic fathering is God's antidote to the orphan spirit. Without it, the Church produces attenders, not disciples; fans, not sons.

Equipping the Saints, Not Entertaining the Saints

Apostolic leadership carries the mandate to equip, not entertain. Paul wrote that the five-fold gifts exist so that *"we all come in the unity of the faith, and of the knowledge of the Son of God, unto a perfect man, unto the measure of the stature of the fulness of Christ"* (Ephesians 4:13).

Entertainment produces applause; equipping produces armies. A crowd can be stirred, but only disciples can be sent. If your people can cheer but cannot minister, you've built an audience, not an army.

Equipping means training believers to discern, to pray, to heal the sick, to cast out demons, and to proclaim the gospel. Paul reminded Timothy: *"All scripture is given by inspiration of God, and is profitable… that the man of God may be perfect, throughly furnished unto all good works"* (2 Timothy 3:16–17). Apostolic leaders teach the Word until the people are furnished for battle.

Jesus modeled this perfectly. He never called men to spectate but to follow, to deny themselves, to take up the cross. He trained disciples who carried His power into the world. Apostolic leaders restore that pattern.

Authority to Build, Not Control

Apostolic authority is real, but it is never tyrannical. Paul wrote: *"For though I should boast somewhat more of our authority, which the Lord hath given us for edification, and not for your destruction, I should not be ashamed"* (2 Corinthians 10:8). Authority is given to build, not break; to strengthen, not manipulate.

Hebrews 13:17 instructs believers: *"Obey them that have the rule over you, and submit yourselves: for they watch for your souls, as they that must give account."* Apostolic authority carries a holy weight - leaders will give account for how they shepherd.

Authority is not for ego - it's for execution of heaven's blueprint.

Apostolic authority is not about control - it's about construction. Jesus said in Matthew 20:26, *"Whosoever will be great among you, let him be your minister."*

Apostolic authority bows to serve, not to dominate. It washes feet, it heals wounds, it lays down life for the sheep

If your authority tears people down, it is not apostolic - it is carnal.

Fathers vs. Hirelings

The difference between an apostle and a hireling is the difference between a father and a manager. Paul told the Corinthians: *"For though ye have ten thousand instructors in Christ, yet have ye not many fathers: for in Christ Jesus I have begotten you through the gospel"* (1 Corinthians 4:15).

Hirelings gather crowds but never reproduce legacy. Jesus warned: *"He that is an hireling, and not the shepherd, whose own the sheep are not, seeth the wolf coming, and leaveth the sheep, and fleeth"* (John 10:12–13).

Hirelings build events; fathers build legacies. Hirelings count heads; fathers raise sons. A hireling looks for numbers; a father looks for inheritance.

Fathers invest their lives into people who will one day surpass them. Apostolic fathers rejoice when their sons do greater works. Malachi 4:6 promised generational reconciliation - the turning of fathers' hearts to children and children's hearts to fathers. Without this fathering, the land is struck with a curse. Apostolic leadership is God's answer.

Order Brings Fruitfulness

Where there is no apostolic order, chaos reigns. Where order is restored, fruitfulness multiplies. Paul wrote to Titus: *"For this cause left I thee in Crete, that thou shouldest set in order the things that are wanting, and ordain elders in every city"* (Titus 1:5).

Order is not legalism; it is the environment where fruit can flourish. Paul reminded the Corinthians: *"Let all things be done decently and in order"* (1 Corinthians 14:40).

Chaos never multiplies; it divides. Order is the seedbed of reproduction. Disorder drains strength; order multiplies it.

Genesis 1 shows this principle. The earth was *"without form, and void"* (Genesis 1:2). But when God spoke order - light from darkness, land from water - fruitfulness appeared. Apostolic order does the same in the Church: it turns barrenness into harvest.

Acts 16:5 shows the result: *"So were the churches established in the faith, and increased in number daily."* Establishment in order always precedes multiplication in growth.

Prophetic Insight: Restoring Apostolic Leadership in This Generation

This generation is crying out for fathers, not hirelings. For builders, not entertainers. For leaders who carry authority with humility, order with compassion, and vision with sacrifice.

Prophetic insight that roars: The orphan spirit will not be broken until apostolic fathers rise again. The Church will not mature until it is led by builders, not performers.

Ephesians 4:14 warns that without this equipping, believers remain *"children, tossed to and fro, and carried about with every wind of doctrine."* Apostolic leadership anchors believers in maturity and guards them from deception.

A prophetic warning: If you cannot reproduce, you are only renting the future.

Apostolic leadership thinks generationally. It multiplies sons and daughters who will carry the torch further.

The call is clear: God is restoring apostolic fathers who will raise up sons and daughters, not slaves or spectators.

Practical Application for Leaders and Churches

1. Equip, Don't Entertain. Measure success not by applause but by how many are equipped for ministry (Ephesians 4:11–12; 2 Timothy 3:16–17).

2. Use Authority to Build. Exercise authority only to edify, never to dominate (2 Corinthians 10:8; Hebrews 13:17). Authority is not for ego - it is for execution of heaven's blueprint.

3. Be a Father, Not a Hireling. Invest in people as sons, not as statistics (1 Corinthians 4:15; John 10:12–13; Malachi 4:5–6).

4. Set Order in the House. Establish governance and discipline (Titus 1:5; 1 Corinthians 14:40). Order precedes fruit.

5. Multiply Legacy. Train others to surpass you. Acts 16:5 shows churches established and increasing daily. If your ministry dies with you, it was ambition, not apostolic.

6. Walk in Humility. Apostolic authority looks like washing feet (John 13:14–15).

Conclusion: A Call to Apostolic Order

The Church in this hour desperately needs apostolic leadership restored. Not as titles on business cards, but as fathers in the house of God. Not as celebrities on stages, but as builders in the trenches.

A prophetic call has gone forth: "The days of orphan churches are over. The Lord is raising fathers to build families, apostles to set order, and leaders to reproduce sons.

Only when apostolic order is restored will the Church rise in maturity, walk in unity, and advance in power. The harvest is waiting, but the harvest requires fathers.

Scripture Index

- Ephesians 2:20
- Ephesians 4:11–14
- 1 Corinthians 3:10
- 1 Corinthians 4:15
- 1 Corinthians 14:40
- 2 Corinthians 10:8
- Titus 1:5
- Matthew 20:26
- John 10:12–13
- John 13:14–15
- Genesis 1:2–3
- Acts 16:5
- Hebrews 13:17
- 2 Timothy 3:16–17
- Malachi 4:5–6

Chapter Twenty-Two

A Vision for Generations – Raising Successors and Building a Church That Lasts

Introduction: The Mandate of Continuity

Every genuine move of God demands more than one generation. The Kingdom is never entrusted to a single man, a single age group, or a single lifetime. It is built to outlast us. Psalm 78:4–6 declares: *"We will not hide them from their children, shewing to the generation to come the praises of the LORD, and his strength, and his wonderful works that he hath done… That the generation to come might know them, even the children which should be born; who should arise and declare them to their children."*

The vision of God is never a snapshot; it is a scroll, rolled open over decades, carried in the hands of sons and daughters yet unborn. The Spirit of God is raising a people who think generationally - who understand that the flame of revival is not preserved in glass but passed hand to hand, from heart to heart, until the Lord returns.

Deuteronomy 6:6–7 commands: *"These words, which I command thee this day, shall be in thine heart: And thou shalt teach them diligently unto thy children."* Joel 1:3 echoes: *"Tell ye your children of it, and let your children tell their children, and their children another generation."*

218

Prophetic declarations rise in this hour:

- The Kingdom is not built on monuments to the past but on mantles carried into the future
- The testimony of one generation is the inheritance of the next.
- If you do not declare it, your children cannot inherit it.

Raising Successors, Not Hoarding Positions

Too many cling to titles and pulpits as if the Church were their possession. But the Kingdom cannot be hoarded - it must be handed off. Paul told Timothy: *"The things that thou hast heard of me among many witnesses, the same commit thou to faithful men, who shall be able to teach others also"* (2 Timothy 2:2).

Here is the unbroken line: Paul → Timothy → faithful men → those they will teach. Four generations of faith in one verse. This is how the Kingdom advances - through succession, not possession.

Moses prepared Joshua to cross into the promise. Elijah left his mantle for Elisha, and Elisha cried out, *"My father, my father, the chariot of Israel, and the horsemen thereof"* (2 Kings 2:12). Jesus poured Himself into the Twelve, and Paul raised Timothy and

Titus. Fathers rejoiced when sons surpassed them. True leadership is proven not by what you do, but by what lives on after you.

Malachi 4:6 warns: *"And he shall turn the heart of the fathers to the children, and the heart of the children to their fathers, lest I come and smite the earth with a curse."* Proverbs 13:22 adds: *"A good man leaveth an inheritance to his children's children."*

Prophetic insights:

- To fail to raise successors is to betray the future.
- A leader who dies with everything in his hands dies with empty hands.
- Your mantle is not proof of greatness until another generation wears it.

Building Legacy Through Family and Army

The vision of God's house is always family first, then army. Abram raised a household of trained servants who became warriors in Genesis 14:14. The local church is God's family that matures into God's army. Sons and daughters become soldiers, and soldiers carry inheritance.

Psalm 127:3–5 declares: *"Lo, children are an heritage of the LORD: and the fruit of the womb is his reward. As arrows are in the hand of a mighty man; so are children of the youth. Happy is the man that hath his quiver full of them."* Children - biological and spiritual - are arrows launched into the future.

But an army without succession is vulnerable, and a family without sons and daughters to inherit becomes extinct. Ephesians 6:10–13 reminds us: *"Be strong in the Lord, and in the power of his might… put on the whole armour of God, that ye may be able to stand against the wiles of the devil."*

Prophetic declarations rise:

- You cannot call yourself a general if you leave behind no army.
- You cannot call yourself a father if you leave behind no sons.
- The family must grow into an army, and the army must build legacy.

Generational Continuity: From Family to Army to Legacy

Psalm 145:4 declares: *"One generation shall praise thy works to another, and shall declare thy mighty acts."* The Kingdom is designed for continuity. When fathers raise sons, when generals train soldiers, when leaders hand off legacy, the pattern of God moves forward unhindered.

But when the cycle is broken, decline comes swiftly. Judges 2:10 says: *"And also all that generation were gathered unto their fathers: and there arose another generation after them, which knew not the LORD, nor yet the works which he had done for Israel.*" One untrained generation, one neglected succession, one failure of inheritance - and the knowledge of God can vanish from a land.

The pattern is clear:

- Family gathers and nurtures.

- Army trains and sends.

- Legacy multiplies and sustains.

When this cycle is intact, the Church becomes unstoppable. When it is broken, the flame sputters and dies.

Prophetic declarations:

- The fire must not go out on your watch.

- What you refuse to pass on will be buried with you.

- Legacy is not memory - it is multiplication.

Prophetic Insight: The Eternal Torch

The Spirit speaks: Do not allow the flame to die in your generation. What I placed in you is not for you alone; it is for the generations after you.

The Lord Himself sent fire from heaven to ignite the altar that was commanded to be built. But after it burned, He gave this eternal command: *"The fire shall ever be burning upon the altar; it shall never go out."* (Leviticus 6:13)

God was the One who lit the flame - but He placed the responsibility of "maintaining it" in our hands. His fire is not a one-time visitation; it is a perpetual covenant of communion. Every generation must tend the flame. We are the priests of this age, commanded to keep the fire burning -through worship, prayer, and obedience - so that no generation will ever stand before a cold altar again. This is what we leave for the next generation.

Elijah left his mantle for Elisha. Paul left his letters for the Church. Jesus left His Spirit for us all. The Kingdom is an unbroken chain of testimony, each link forged in fire. Hebrews 12:1–2 reminds us that we are surrounded by *"so great a cloud of witnesses... looking unto Jesus the author and finisher of our faith."*

The torch is in your hand, but it will not remain there forever. One day, you must pass it on. And when you do, may it burn brighter, not dimmer. For the Kingdom does not diminish with time - it multiplies.

Haggai 2:9 promises: *"The glory of this latter house shall be greater than of the former."*

Prophetic insights:

- The torch you carry is not for you to admire - it is for you to release.

- If your fire ends with you, it was ambition. If your fire multiplies, it was Kingdom.

- The testimony of fathers becomes the fuel of sons.

Practical Application: How to Build a Church That Lasts

1. Train Successors Intentionally. Do not wait for a crisis. Raise them now. (2 Timothy 2:2).

2. Think Generationally. Build with decades in mind, not weeks. (Psalm 78:6).

3. Release Inheritance. Share authority, wisdom, and opportunity. (1 Corinthians 4:15).

4. Build Family Before Army. Sons must know they are loved before they are sent. (Genesis 14:14).

5. Guard the Flame. Never allow the testimony of God's works to be forgotten. (Psalm 78:4).

6. Teach Diligently. Deuteronomy 6:7 commands teaching children at all times.

7. Invest in Arrows. Psalm 127:4–5 - children are arrows to be launched into the future.

8. Pass the Mantle Boldly. 2 Kings 2:9–10 - Elisha asked for a double portion, and it was granted.

9. Stay Faithful Until the End. Hebrews 12:2 - look unto Jesus, the author and finisher.

Prophetic reminders:

- If you fail to disciple, the world will.
- Every arrow you launch shapes a generation you may never see.
- Legacy is not built in one day, but it can be lost in one day of neglect.

Conclusion: A Vision for Generations

The call of Chapter 20 is clear: see beyond yourself. Build for generations yet unborn. Declare His works to your children's children. Raise successors who will stand when you are gone.

The Kingdom is not a sprint - it is a relay. Each runner carries the baton for a season, then passes it forward. If one runner drops it, the race falters. But when each is faithful, the finish is sure.

Isaiah 9:7 declares: *"Of the increase of his government and peace there shall be no end."* Revelation 11:15 resounds: *"The kingdoms of this world are become the kingdoms of our Lord, and of his Christ; and he shall reign for ever and ever."*

The Spirit cries:

- Lift your eyes beyond your years.
- Build not for applause but for inheritance.

- Raise sons, train daughters, release mantles, guard the flame.
- For I am a God of legacy, and My Church shall outlast every throne of men, every empire of Babylon, and every kingdom of this world.

The Church began in fire, and she will finish in fire. The torch is in your hand. Pass it on.

A final prophetic word of clarity: You don't need to sow money into some distant ministry to receive revelation, deliverance, or healing. These are covenant rights, and they should flow freely from your own local church - the house where God has planted you if it was built correctly.

Scripture index

- Hebrews 12:1–2
- Proverbs 22:6
- Leviticus 6:13

- Isaiah 9:7
- Revelation 11:1

Chapter Twenty-Three

The Multiplication of Fathers and Mothers

Raising Generations, Not Building Thrones

A local church is not the kingdom of one man. It is the family of many fathers. It is not the echo of one voice but the symphony of many who have walked with God. The idea that only one person can be the "father" of a house is not Kingdom order - it is spiritual monopoly disguised as loyalty. Paul dismantled this illusion when he wrote, *"For though ye have ten thousand instructors in Christ, yet have ye not many fathers"* (1 Corinthians 4:15). Notice - he didn't say "only one father." He said "not many," meaning true fatherhood is rare, but not exclusive. God never limits His sons to one source of impartation. He multiplies fatherhood across generations so that His sons and daughters grow balanced, healthy, and whole. When God raises many fathers, He is not causing confusion - He is revealing "completeness." Just as a child learns mathematics from one teacher, language from another, and character from the home, so believers mature through many fathers, each releasing a unique portion of grace. The Kingdom pattern is not "control;" it is "collaboration." True fathers and mothers understand that their sons and daughters must grow beyond their own shadow. They do not build walls of ownership - they build bridges of impartation.

False Fatherhood: The Spirit of Control

Every time God raises fathers, the enemy raises counterfeits. False fatherhood produces dependency, not destiny. It demands loyalty without legacy. It builds personal kingdoms while neglecting the King's Kingdom.

Jesus confronted this mindset directly when He said, *"Call no man your father upon the earth: for one is your Father, which is in heaven"* (Matthew 23:9). He was not abolishing spiritual relationships - He was confronting the spirit of control that seeks to replace the Father Himself.

When a leader insists, "I am your only father, or only pastor" he begins to compete with God's sovereignty. That voice becomes an idol, and the people under it stop hearing the voice of the true Father. Spiritual control replaces covenant relationship. Sons become slaves. Honor becomes hierarchy.

But in the true Kingdom order, fathers release, not restrain. They guide without dominating. They correct without caging. Their authority flows from love, not fear. A real father does not say, "You can't grow beyond me." A true father declares, "You must surpass me."

The Pattern of Paul: Multiplying Sons Across Cities

Paul carried a father's heart that transcended geography. He called Timothy his son (1 Timothy 1:2), Titus his son (Titus

1:4), and even the church in Corinth his beloved children (1 Corinthians 4:14). Yet he never demanded exclusivity. Each son was unique. Each carried a part of his mantle.

Paul's fatherhood was "apostolic, not possessive." He trained Timothy for endurance, Titus for order, and Philemon for restoration. Different sons, same heart, multiplied across cities. This is the model of the New Testament Church - fathers reproducing fathers, not followers.

He taught Timothy, *"The things that thou hast heard of me among many witnesses, the same commit thou to faithful men, who shall be able to teach others also"* (2 Timothy 2:2). That verse carries four generations of spiritual fatherhood: Paul → Timothy → faithful men → others also. Kingdom fatherhood multiplies generations. It never ends with one man; it extends through lineage. The Kingdom does not raise monuments - it raises men. It does not build empires - it builds families that outlive the founders.

The Collaboration of Fathers and Mothers

In the Kingdom, fatherhood is not limited to gender. The Spirit raises fathers and mothers who together nurture, correct, and strengthen the household of faith. Paul described his leadership with both tenderness and strength: *"We were gentle among you, even as a nurse cherisheth her children... as a father doth his children, exhorting and comforting you"* (1 Thessalonians 2:7, 1 Thessalonians

2:11). Notice the balance - motherly nurture and fatherly charge. Both are needed to produce healthy generations.

Fathers impart strength; mothers impart nurture. Fathers train; mothers sustain. Fathers build; mothers birth. The local church needs both to function as the family of God. Without fathers, the church lacks authority. Without mothers, it lacks compassion. Together, they reveal the heart of the Father - the God who both commands and comforts, who disciplines and delights.

The Restoration of Generational Flow

The enemy's strategy has always been to break the flow between generations - to replace fathers with instructors, and sons with orphans. But the Spirit of Elijah is rising again to restore what religion fractured. *"And he shall turn the heart of the fathers to the children, and the heart of the children to their fathers"* (Malachi 4:6). This prophecy is not about sentiment - it's about structure. It is the restoration of generational order in the house of God. When fathers reconnect with sons, blessing returns. When sons honor fathers, legacy multiplies. When mothers restore daughters, inheritance flows freely again. This is not nostalgia - it is Kingdom government being reestablished. The family of God is Heaven's administration on earth. When fathers and mothers rise, the orphan spirit dies.

Conclusion: Many Fathers, One Kingdom

The church was never meant to be a one-man empire. It was meant to be a many-fathered family under one heavenly Father. The Kingdom is not sustained by celebrity - it is built by covenant. A local church may have one senior leader, but it must have many fathers and mothers - voices of wisdom, pillars of strength, and hearts that nurture the generations. For though you may have ten thousand teachers, you still need fathers. And though you may have many fathers, there is only one Father of all, who is above all, through all, and in all (Ephesians 4:6). Let every father rise. Let every mother be restored. Let every son and daughter find their place. For the Kingdom advances not through performance, but through parenthood. Not through one man's control, but through a family's covenant. This is the order of Heaven - the multiplication of fathers, the maturing of sons, and the manifestation of the Kingdom on earth.

When God raises many fathers, He is not causing confusion - He is revealing completeness. Just as a child learns mathematics from one teacher, language from another, and character from the home, so believers mature through many fathers, each releasing a unique portion of grace.

The Kingdom pattern is not control; it is collaboration. True fathers and mothers understand that their sons and daughters must grow beyond their own shadow. They do not build walls of ownership - they build bridges of impartation.

232

Scripture Index

Conclusion

The Kingdom That Cannot Be Shaken

Introduction: The Mandate of Continuity

The time has come for the builders to stand again. The shaking that sweeps across the earth is not to destroy the house of God - it is to reveal what was truly built upon the Rock. Everything that can be shaken will be shaken, so that what cannot be shaken may remain. The kingdoms of men crumble, but the Kingdom of God endures forever. *"Yet once more I shake not the earth only, but also heaven... that those things which cannot be shaken may remain"* (Hebrews 12:26–27)

Through every storm, through every testing, the local church has been God's embassy of hope - His dwelling place among men. The family that became an army now stands as a fortress of light in a generation consumed by darkness. These walls are not made of brick or mortar; they are living stones - hearts redeemed by blood, lives bound together by covenant, voices unified in worship.

When the world looks for stability, it must see it in us. When nations falter, they must find a people whose hope is anchored in eternity. The Church is not hiding; it is advancing. The Bride is not retreating; she is being refined. The Spirit of God is raising up Nehemiahs, Ezras, and Deborahs - builders who refuse to bow to Babylon, who see beyond temporary applause and build with eternity in view.

A Church Built for Glory

This generation was never called to entertain - it was called to build. Programs will fade. Trends will pass. But a house built on the Word and filled with the Spirit will carry glory that outlives empires. *"The glory of this latter house shall be greater than the former"* (Haggai 2:9).

Every stone laid in obedience becomes part of an eternal structure. Every act of faith, every hidden intercession, every unseen tear is mortar in the walls of God's habitation. Builders may go unnoticed by men, but heaven records every stroke of their labor. For the day is coming when *"fire shall try every man's work of what sort it is"* (1 Corinthians 3:13). Only what is built on Christ will endure.

Let the Church rise - not as a crowd of spectators, but as a company of soldiers. Let the sound of worship and warfare echo again. Let the testimonies of deliverance fill the altars. Let fathers raise sons and mothers raise daughters. Let the Bride prepare herself for her returning King.

The Lord is rebuilding His Church - not with celebrities, but with servants. Not with audiences, but with armies. The

Church that will shake nations is not the one most applauded but the one most aligned.

The Hope That Anchors

Hope is not fragile optimism - it is the anchor of the soul. When all else fails, hope holds fast. *"This hope we have as an anchor of the soul, both sure and steadfast"* (Hebrews 6:19).

There is hope for the weary builder, hope for the broken shepherd, hope for the fallen leader. The hands that trembled under the weight of the work will yet lift again. The God who called you has not changed His mind. The same Spirit that raised Jesus from the dead still quickens mortal men to finish what He began.

"Fear not, little flock; for it is your Father's good pleasure to give you the kingdom" (Luke 12:32). The Kingdom will not end in defeat. The gates of hell will not prevail. The same power that began the Church in Acts will bring her to glory in Revelation. The Spirit and the Bride still say, "Come."

A Vision That Outlives You

The Kingdom was never designed to orbit one man; it was designed to multiply generations. Fathers and mothers raise sons and daughters; sons and daughters become fathers and mothers in turn. Legacy is the language of heaven.

Paul told Timothy, *"The things that thou hast heard of me among many witnesses, the same commit thou to faithful men, who shall be able to teach others also"* (2 Timothy 2:2). This is the fourfold rhythm of Kingdom succession: impartation, activation, multiplication, continuation.

Our vision must outlive us. Our call must echo beyond our lifetime. Let the pastors who read these pages raise builders who will outbuild them. Let the prophets train voices stronger than their own. Let the apostles lay foundations for a generation yet unborn.

We are not building monuments; we are building movements. The Church that Jesus builds is not a memory - it is a living lineage of faith that carries His name into every century until He returns.

The Blessed Hope

All creation groans for this moment - the revealing of the sons and daughters of God. *"For the earnest expectation of the creature waiteth for the manifestation of the sons of God"* (Romans 8:19). The Spirit is still brooding over the earth, awakening sons, restoring daughters, reviving churches, rebuilding altars, and renewing hope.

There is a river whose streams make glad the city of God. It flows through every generation that dares to believe, every church that dares to build, every saint that dares to stand.

And when the final trumpet sounds, and the Son of Man returns in glory, He will not find a Church cowering in compromise but a Bride radiant with righteousness, a Kingdom that has endured every shaking and stands unmovable, unshaken, unashamed.

The Final Call of Hope

So rise, builder of the Kingdom. Strengthen your hands again. Stand shoulder to shoulder with your brothers and sisters. The blueprint has not changed. The foundation is sure. The Cornerstone remains.

The Church is marching forward - not in defeat but in dominion, not in fear but in faith. The Lion of Judah is roaring again through His people. The days of lukewarm religion are over; the hour of Kingdom manifestation is here.

Let the redeemed declare: "The Lord is building His house, and the glory shall fill it."

Lift your eyes, for the King is coming. The Spirit and the Bride say, Come.

Scripture References

- Hebrews 12:26–27
- Haggai 2:9
- 1 Corinthians 3:13
- Hebrews 6:19
- Luke 12:32
- Romans 8:19

- 2 Timothy 2:2
- Psalm 78:4
- Revelation 22:17
- Ephesians 2:21–22

Glossary

of Theological and Kingdom Terms

Apostolic Alignment

Positioning believers under divine order for function and flow in Kingdom purpose. (Ephesians 2:20; 1 Corinthians 3:10)

Apostolic Family

A covenant community united by purpose and governed through love and authority. (Acts 2:42–47)

Apostolic Government

Divine leadership structure through apostles and prophets, ensuring alignment and order. (Titus 1:5; 1 Corinthians 12:28)

Audience-Driven Church

A congregation centered on entertainment rather than transformation. (2 Timothy 4:3)

Babylonian System

The world's counterfeit order that replaces God's government with carnal control. (Revelation 18:4)

Bishop (Overseer)

Elders entrusted with oversight and spiritual care of God's people.
(1 Peter 5:2–3)

Builder's Mandate

The divine call to construct God's house in obedience to
revelation. (Nehemiah 2:18)

Church Government

The spiritual order of authority within the Church led by fivefold
ministry. (Ephesians 4:11–13)

Corporate Anointing

The multiplied power of unity when believers align in obedience.
(Psalm 133:1–3)

Covenant Family

A spiritual household bound by covenant and shared purpose.
(Acts 2:44–47)

Deacon (Servant-Leader)

Spirit-filled servant operating under apostolic direction for
practical ministry. (Acts 6:3–7)

Delegated Authority

The power to act on behalf of Christ under His commission.
(Luke 10:19)

Ekklesia

The governing assembly of believers representing Heaven's rule
on Earth. (Matthew 16:18–19)

Elder

A mature believer who provides wisdom, stability, and oversight.
(1 Timothy 5:17)

Fivefold Ministry

Five offices equipping believers: apostle, prophet, evangelist,
pastor, teacher. (Ephesians 4:11–13)

Foundation Stones

Core doctrines and principles upholding Kingdom structure.
(Hebrews 6:1–2)

Generational Transfer

Passing spiritual inheritance through relationship and obedience.
(2 Kings 2:9–15)

Kingdom Architecture

Heaven's design for how congregations and ministries are built.
(Ephesians 2:19–22)

Kingdom Authority

Delegated power of Christ exercised through obedient believers.
(Matthew 28:18–20)

Kingdom Culture

The lifestyle and values expressing Heaven's environment on
Earth. (Romans 14:17)

Kingdom Economics

Heaven's system of stewardship and multiplication through
generosity. (Malachi 3:10)

Kingdom-Minded Leadership

Leadership guided by eternal purpose, humility, and legacy. (2
Timothy 2:2)

Living Stones

Believers fitly joined together as the temple of God. (1 Peter 2:5)

Mantle Bearers

Individuals carrying spiritual assignments through inherited grace.
(2 Kings 2:13–15)

Mercenary Spirit

Serving for reward rather than relationship; ministry for gain not
alignment. (John 10:12–13)

Ministry Infrastructure

Organizational frame that supports vision and stewardship. (Mark
2:22)

Obedience Is Not Optional

Faith proven through immediate and complete response to God –
not man. (1 Samuel 15:22)

Prophetic Alignment

Proper positioning for prophetic words to manifest accurately.
(Amos 3:7)

Prophetic Blueprint

Heaven's pattern guiding how the Church should build and move.
(Exodus 25:9)

Prophetic Garden

Spiritual environment where revelation and obedience bear fruit. (Genesis 2:15)

Prophetic Mantle

Covering of revelation and authority transferred through service. (1 Kings 19:19)

Prophetic Protocol

Guidelines ensuring purity and accountability in prophetic ministry. (1 Corinthians 14:29–33)

Prophetic Seasons

God-appointed times for change, growth, and manifestation. (Ecclesiastes 3:1)

Prophetic Voice

Messenger carrying Heaven's message for correction and alignment. (Jeremiah 1:9–10)

Remnant

Faithful minority preserved to rebuild what others have forsaken. (Romans 11:5)

Servant Leadership

Leadership modeled after Christ's humility and service. (John
13:14–15)

Shepherd-Overseer

Pastor leading through love and humility rather than control.
(Ezekiel 34:11–12)

Spirit-Filled Communication

Speech governed by the Holy Spirit that builds and restores.
(Ephesians 4:29)

Spirit-Governed Order

Structure directed by the Holy Spirit, balancing power and peace.
(Romans 8:14)

Spirit-Led Training

Equipping believers by Word and Spirit for active service. (2
Timothy 2:2–3)

Spiritual Architecture

The invisible framework of divine order in people and ministries.
(Hebrews 11:10)

Spiritual Blueprint

The unique divine plan for every believer's life and purpose.
(Psalm 139:16)

Spiritual Fatherhood and Motherhood

Imparting identity and maturity through relationship and example.
(1 Corinthians 4:15)

Synergy of the Spirit

Divine cooperation that multiplies Kingdom effectiveness.
(Deuteronomy 32:30)

The King's Blueprint

Christ's master plan for the structure and expansion of His
Church. (Matthew 16:18)

The Orphan Spirit

An orphan spirit is produced when fathers and leaders in the
house refuse to recognize, receive, or release the sons and
daughters God has raised or sent. It is birthed in
environments where control replaces covenant, where
manipulation smothers maturity, and where leaders cling
to authority instead of cultivating it in others. (Romans
8:15)

The Spirit of Religion

Form without power; replacing intimacy with ritual. (2 Corinthians
3:6)

Theocracy

Government of God through His chosen leadership structure.
(Isaiah 33:22)

Truth That Divides

The Word of God that separates compromise from conviction.
(Hebrews 4:12)

Unified Command

Collective leadership moving in synchronized obedience.
(Philippians 2:2)

Vision Carriers

Faithful supporters of divine vision through loyalty and maturity.
(Habakkuk 2:2–3)

Wise Counsel

Discernment from mature voices preserving direction and purity.
(Proverbs 11:14)

Wise Master Builder

Leader who builds foundations with divine wisdom and order. (1
Corinthians 3:10)

Worship as Lifestyle

Daily surrender that expresses love beyond song. (Romans 12:1–2)

Zion Order

Divine arrangement of worship and government revealing
Heaven's glory. (Isaiah 2:2–3)

Appendix I

This appendix was added for the discerning reader who desires not only references but fuller revelation - where Scripture and theology are not merely cited but unfolded. Here, you can explore a deeper, unfiltered look into the prelude itself and the scriptures used for development.

Prelude with additional references

His glory; the earth displayed His design *(Psalm 19:1–2)*. Man was not created to attend a service, but to host His presence - to be the living sanctuary of the Almighty in the midst of creation *(1 Corinthians 3:16; 2 Corinthians 6:16)*.

When man fell, heaven did not abandon earth - it began to build again. From the ruins of rebellion, the Father drafted a new blueprint of redemption *(Genesis 3:15; Isaiah 9:6–7)*. Every covenant was a construction phase *(Genesis 12:2–3; Exodus 19:5–6)*, every prophet a builder *(Haggai 1:8; Amos 9:11)*, every apostle a foreman of destiny *(Ephesians 2:20; 1 Corinthians 3:10)*. The altar of Abraham, the tabernacle of Moses, the temple of Solomon - all were foundations pointing to something greater *(Hebrews 8:5; 9:11–12)*. Then came the Master Builder Himself - Christ, the Son of the Living God - declaring, *"Upon this rock I will build My Church, and the gates of hell shall not prevail against it." (Matthew 16:18)*

The local church, therefore, is not an invention of man; it is the continuation of that divine construction. It is the visible blueprint of the invisible Kingdom *(Luke 17:20–21)*. It is the training ground where sons and daughters are forged into builders *(Ephesians 4:11–13)*, where family becomes army *(Genesis 14:14; Ephesians 6:10–18)*, and where obedience becomes architecture *(James 1:22; Matthew 7:24)*. Every sermon is a stone *(1 Peter 2:5)*. Every act of discipleship, a beam. Every transformed life, a wall rising toward heaven's vision.

The Pattern of the Builder

Every generation is tested by whether it will preserve the pattern. Heaven's designs are never suggestions; they are sacred trust.

Moses was warned, *"See that thou make all things according to the pattern shewed to thee in the mount." (Hebrews 8:5; Exodus 25:9, 40)*. Paul echoed that same call: *"As a wise master builder, I have laid the foundation." (1 Corinthians 3:10)*.

The pattern has not changed. Apostles and prophets lay the foundation *(Ephesians 2:20)*. Evangelists, pastors, and teachers build upon it *(Ephesians 4:11–12)*. Each member of the body fits together as living stones, chosen and shaped by the hand of the Builder Himself *(1 Peter 2:4–6)*. When the pattern is followed, the glory fills the house *(2 Chronicles 7:1–3; Haggai 2:7–9)*. When it is ignored, Ichabod is written over the door *(1 Samuel 4:21–22)*.

252

This is why the enemy wages his fiercest war against the local church *(Acts 20:29–30)*. He fears not our gatherings, but our unity *(Psalm 133:1–3; John 17:21–23)*. He trembles when the people of God build in order, aligned with apostolic blueprints and prophetic fire. Babylon builds towers to make names for men *(Genesis 11:4)*; Zion builds temples to reveal the name of the King *(Psalm 48:1–3; Isaiah 2:2–3)*. One is confusion; the other is glory. One ends in scattering; the other ends in habitation *(Ephesians 2:22)*.

The true church is not a monument to human achievement but a movement of divine government *(Isaiah 9:7; Daniel 7:27)*. Its leaders are not executives but fathers and mothers *(1 Corinthians 4:15; 1 Thessalonians 2:7–11)*. Its members are not customers but soldiers of covenant *(2 Timothy 2:3–4)*. The church exists not to host performances but to host Presence *(Exodus 33:14–15; John 14:23)* - because when God dwells among His people, every power of darkness begins to crumble *(Psalm 97:5; Mark 1:27)*.

The Mandate to Build

The Spirit of the Lord is issuing the same command that stirred Nehemiah's heart in ancient ruins: *"Let us rise up and build."* *(Nehemiah 2:18)*

This is not a suggestion for the talented - it is a mandate for the obedient *(Haggai 1:8)*. Heaven is not impressed by motion but by momentum, not by numbers but by transformation *(Romans*

12:2). We have built enough stages; it is time to build altars *(1 Kings 18:30–32)*. We have measured success by attendance; heaven measures by obedience *(1 Samuel 15:22; Matthew 7:21)*. We have polished our performances; it is time to forge disciples *(Matthew 28:19–20)*.

The Church is not the waiting room for heaven; it is the workshop of the Kingdom *(Matthew 25:14–30)*. Every act of faithfulness lays another stone *(1 Corinthians 15:58)*. Every disciple raised strengthens another wall *(Isaiah 58:12)*. Every family healed extends the perimeter of heaven's domain on earth *(Matthew 6:10)*. When believers take their place as builders, the earth begins to mirror the government of heaven *(Habakkuk 2:14)*.

The blueprint is not hidden - it is written in the Word *(Psalm 119:89)*. The Cornerstone is not uncertain - it is Christ alone *(Ephesians 2:20; 1 Peter 2:6–7)*. The call is not for a few - it is for all who bear His name *(Acts 2:39)*. The Kingdom will not be built by entertainment but by endurance *(2 Timothy 4:2–5)*, not by charisma but by covenant *(Deuteronomy 7:9)*, not by applause but by alignment with heaven's pattern *(Romans 8:29–30)*.

From Foundation to Fulfillment

The day is coming when the final stone will be set and the heavenly voice will thunder again: *"Behold, the tabernacle of God is with men." (Revelation 21:3)*

In that moment, every local church built in obedience will echo in eternity *(1 Corinthians 15:58; Revelation 14:13)*. Every hidden labor, every unseen prayer, every act of sacrifice will become part of the eternal architecture of the New Jerusalem *(Hebrews 11:10, 16)*. The Bride will stand complete - glorious, united, and radiant with the light of the Lamb *(Revelation 21:9–11)*. The King's blueprint will be finished.

So lift your eyes, builder of the Kingdom. Your hammer is your obedience *(James 2:17)*. Your nails are your prayers *(Ephesians 6:18)*. Your material is the living stones sitting beside you *(1 Peter 2:5)*. The foundation has been laid, and the Cornerstone holds firm *(Isaiah 28:16; 1 Corinthians 3:11)*.

The voice of the Builder still calls through time: *"Rise up and build." (Nehemiah 2:18)* For what you build now will stand when heaven and earth have passed away *(Matthew 24:35)*. The kingdoms of men will crumble *(Daniel 2:44–45)*, but the Kingdom built through the local church will endure forever *(Psalm 145:13; Hebrews 12:28)*.

Index

Thematic

259

Scripture Index

Old Testament

265

266

New Testament

271

Bibliography

Hersey, P., & Blanchard, K. H. (1977). *Situational Leadership: Adapting Leadership Styles to Followers' Maturity.* Addison Wesley.

Luther, M. (1962). *Ninety-five Theses.* Anchoe Books.

Tuckman, B. W. (1965). Developmental Sequence in Small Groups. *Psychological Bulletin*, *63*(6), 384–399.

Webb, D. (2025). *The Unique Factor.* Eternal Kingdom International Publishing, LLC.

Other Good Books

from EKI Publishing

- *The Unique Factor*
  - o By David Webb
- *Escape the Shame of Babylon*
  - o By David Webb
- *Building the Kingdom Through the Local Church*
  - o By David Webb
- *Unchained: Freed to be His Treasure*
  - o By Kirkland M. Rite
- *Baptized: Why did I get Wet*
  - o By Kirland M. Rite

Coming from Eternal Kingdom
International Publishing

December 2025

Unchained

By Kirkland M. Rite